Voting Counts:
Electoral Reform
for Canada

LAW COMMISSION OF CANADA
COMMISSION DU DROIT DU CANADA

Ce document est également disponible en français :
Un vote qui compte : la réforme électorale au Canada.
ISBN : J31-61/2004F
Catalogue : 0-662-76208-8

This Report is also available online at www.lcc.gc.ca.

To order a copy of the Report, contact:

Law Commission of Canada
222 Queen Street, Suite 1124
Ottawa ON K1A 0H8
Telephone: (613) 946-8980
Facsimile: (613) 946-8988
E-mail: info@lcc.gc.ca

Cover illustration by David Badour.

Canadä

ISBN: J31-61/2004E
Catalogue: 0-662-36426-0

The Honourable Irwin Cotler
Minister of Justice
Justice Building
Wellington Street
Ottawa, Ontario
K1A 0H8

Dear Minister:

In accordance with section 5(1)(c) of the *Law Commission of Canada Act*, we are pleased to submit the Report of the Law Commission of Canada on reforming the electoral system to ensure that democracy in Canada remains vibrant and relevant into the 21st century.

Yours sincerely,

Nathalie Des Rosiers,
President

Bernard Colas,
Commissioner

Roderick J. Wood,
Commissioner

Mark L. Stevenson,
Commissioner

Table of Contents

Letter of Transmittal i

Preface vii

Acknowledgments ix

Executive Summary xiii

Chapter 1 Introduction 1

    1.1 Canada's Electoral System...1

    1.2 Democratic Reform and Electoral Systems.......................3

    1.3 Concerns with the Status Quo 8

    1.4 Objectives and Organization of this Report 13

Chapter 2 Reviewing Electoral Systems and
                  Reform Proposals in Canada 19

    2.1 Introduction 19

    2.2 Families of Electoral Systems...19
        2.2.1 Plurality–Majority Systems 19
        2.2.2 Proportional Representation Systems 22
        2.2.3 Semi-PR Systems 24

    2.3 Electoral Reform in Canada 26
        2.3.1 Early Reform Efforts...26
        2.3.2 Post-1950 Electoral Reform Concerns 28

    2.4 Current Reform Proposals 31
        2.4.1 Diversity and Representation 33
        2.4.2 Distorted Election Results 37
        2.4.3 Voter Turnout 38
        2.4.4 Youth Participation 40
        2.4.5 International Precedents.......................................42

    2.5 Electoral Reform and the Canadian Political Agenda 43

Chapter 3 Democratic Values and the Choice of Electoral System 53

3.1 Systems and Values 53

3.2 Evaluating Electoral Systems 54

3.3 Criteria for Evaluating Electoral Systems 58
3.3.1 Representation of Parties 59
3.3.2 Demographic Representation 60
3.3.3 Diversity of Ideas 63
3.3.4 Geographic Representation 65
3.3.5 Effective Government 66
3.3.6 Accountable Government 66
3.3.7 Effective Opposition 67
3.3.8 Valuing Votes 67
3.3.9 Regional Balance 69
3.3.10 Inclusive Decision Making 71

3.4 First-past-the-post: Time for Change 72

Chapter 4 Electoral Options for Canada 77

4.1 Balancing Competing Factors 77

4.2 Majoritarian Systems 78
4.2.1 Two-round System 78
4.2.2 Alternative Vote System 79

4.3 Proportional Systems 80
4.3.1 Single Transferable Vote System 80
4.3.2 List-PR System 82

4.4 Mixed Electoral Systems 83
4.4.1 Mixed Member Majoritarian System 85
4.4.2 Mixed Member Proportional System 90
4.4.3 Germany's Mixed Member Proportional System 90
4.4.4 Scotland's Mixed Member Proportional System 94

4.5 Diversity and Representation 104
4.5.1 Open Versus Closed Lists 104
4.5.2 Women's Representation 109
4.5.3 Minority Group Representation 114
4.5.4 Youth Representation 115

4.6 Aboriginal People's Representation in the
New Electoral System..117
    4.6.1 New Zealand 117
    4.6.2 Maine 118
    4.6.3 Royal Commission on Electoral Reform
           and Party Financing...119
    4.6.4 Royal Commission on Aboriginal Peoples...........120

4.7 Electoral System Design Issues 123
    4.7.1 Including Diverse Voices: Thresholds................123
    4.7.2 Accountability: Double Inclusion 125

4.8 Conclusion...126

Chapter 5 Implications of Adding an Element of Proportionality to Canada's Electoral System

**Chapter 5 Implications of Adding an
             Element of Proportionality
             to Canada's Electoral System**...................139

5.1 Introduction...139

5.2 The Impact of Minority or Coalition
    Governments on Political Decision Making 141

5.3 Regionalism..144

5.4 Two "Classes" of Representatives 145

5.5 Government Formation and Accountability 150

5.6 Administrative Costs 152

5.7 Impact on the Public Service......................................152

5.8 Conclusion: Setting the Bar for Electoral Reform.........154

Chapter 6 The Process of Electoral Reform— Engaging Citizens in Democratic Change

**Chapter 6 The Process of Electoral Reform—
             Engaging Citizens in
             Democratic Change** 159

6.1 Electoral Reform and Citizen Engagement..................159

6.2 Support for Democratic Participation
    After Electoral Reform 166

6.3 Conclusion...168

Conclusion   Reforming Electoral
            Democracy in Canada...............................171

Recommendations...175

Appendix A: Creation of Regions within
            Quebec and Ontario for a
            Mixed Member Proportional
            Electoral System 181

Appendix B: Public Consultation and
            Engagement Strategy...............................188

Appendix C: Bibliography...197

Preface

Through the electoral process, citizens grant authority to their governments and to the laws governments enact. In recent years more and more Canadians have expressed their desire for improvements to our system of democratic governance, and to the mechanisms through which they can participate in government decision-making processes.

This Report originated from consultations that the Law Commission of Canada held concerning the challenges facing Canadian law and its institutions. Through these consultations, many Canadians and citizens' groups presented the Commission with their ideas—many of which are embodied in this Report. They argued that it was time to reflect on our democratic aspirations and how they relate to our current electoral system. In short, they suggested that it was time to question whether the existing electoral system continues to meet the democratic goals and needs of Canadian society.

Debates about electoral reform certainly are not new in Canada. At various junctures throughout Canada's history, the electoral system has sparked concern and debate, particularly regarding its ability to adequately translate votes into seats in the legislature, and whether it unfairly rewards large political parties with strong regional support. In recent years, concerns about the voting system have resurfaced, raising new questions about the way in which we elect our political representatives. Reform efforts currently unfolding in several Canadian provinces, and electoral reform movements gathering momentum in civil society, have raised familiar questions about Canada's voting system, as well as highlighted more contemporary concerns about the nature of representation and political participation.

This Report aims to clarify the debates surrounding electoral reform: it reviews the arguments advanced to justify change, evaluates their relevance and cogency, and proposes a new model. It is the culmination of two years of research and consultation by the Commission. The Report benefits greatly from the input the

Commission received from people across Canada, and in other jurisdictions, who are interested in electoral system reform. We hope that this Report will aid the provincial reform initiatives currently taking place, and that it will also stimulate much needed reform debates federally.

Throughout its consultation process, the Commission has heard about how much Canadians care about their democracy; about their desire to participate in the system of governance; and about how seriously they take their role as voters and citizens. They explained why the current system leaves them feeling indifferent and why many do not vote, and they expressed their interest in political participation—in contributing to and energizing Canadian democracy. The many voices heard throughout the engagement process are reflected in this Report. The Commission invites your comments and ideas on the state of Canadian democracy to ensure that it continues to be vibrant and relevant.

Acknowledgments

The Commission thanks the many Canadians who wrote or sent e-mails with their thoughts and feedback, attended our public consultations, provided us with comments on our discussion paper, or used it as part of their group or classroom discussions. The Commission is grateful to these citizens for engaging us on this important issue.

Many scholars and electoral reform researchers inspired this Report. We want to thank Keith Archer, Robert Crocker, Kimberly Earles and Tammy Findlay, Larry Gordon, Ghislain Otis, Dennis Pilon, Brian Schwartz and Darla Rettie, Leslie Seidle, and Manon Tremblay.

During the consultations, the Commission also benefited from working with several organizations and individuals to host special forums, colloquiums and public consultations. A particular thanks goes to Doris Anderson and Larry Gordon (Fair Vote Canada), Barry Turner and Douglas Rowland (Association of Former Parliamentarians), Dave Farthing and Annie Hoang (YouCAN!), Jean-Pierre Kingsley, Diane Davidson, Alain Pelletier, and Leslie Seidle (Elections Canada), Dr. William Cross (Davidson Chair and Director, Centre for Canadian Studies, Mount Allison University and Director of Research, Commission on Legislative Democracy), Jack Jedwab (Association for Canadian Studies), Martine Blanc (Collectif : féminisme et démocratie), Bonnie Diamond (National Association of Women and the Law), Hugh Segal and Geneviève Bouchard (Institute for Research on Public Policy), Dr. Roger Gibbins (Canada West Foundation), Dr. Marsha Hanen and Alison Dempsey (Sheldon M. Chumir Foundation for Ethics in Leadership), Jeannie Lea (Every Vote Counts–Prince Edward Island), Jacques Frémont and Luc Tremblay, (Faculté de droit, Université de Montréal), Wade MacLauchlan and Edward Macdonald (University of Prince Edward Island), Professor Manon Tremblay and Jackie Steele (University of Ottawa, Centre for Research on Women and Politics), Dianne Brydon (Canadian Study of Parliament Group), Margaret Hoff (London Chapter of the Council of Canadians), Rick Odergaard (President's Club, London, Ontario), Margaret McGovern

(Canadian Federation of University Women), Geoff Dinsdale (Canadian Centre for Management Development), Dr. Tsvi Kahana (Centre for Constitutional Studies, University of Alberta), Peter Russell and Andrew McMurtry (Churchill Society for the Advancement of Parliamentary Democracy), Gisèle Yasmeen and Dr. Andrew Parkin (Centre for Research on Information in Canada), and David Daubney.

We also want to thank the people who acted as Moderators and Discussants at our various public consultations: Patrick Boyer, Professor Ed Morgan, Professor Andrew Petter, Professor Richard Johnston, Professor David Smith, Dr. Tsvi Kahana, Professor Grant Huscroft, Professor Paul Nesbitt-Larking, Professor Jennifer Smith, Professor Christopher Waddell, Professor Roderick Macdonald, Mr. Hugh Segal, Mr. Alan Buchanan, Mr. Wade MacLauchlan, Dr. Roger Gibbins, and Dr. Marsha Hanen.

We thank those who participated in our Electoral Reform Study Panel and online discussion group, whose ideas assisted us with our thinking in this Report. Thanks to Jacquie Ackerly, Raj Anand, Professor Darin Barney, Professor André Blais, Geneviève Bouchard, Peter Creighton, Dr. William Cross, Diane Davidson, Jean-Pierre Derriennic, Professor Jane Jenson, Professor Jean Leclair, Professor Heather MacIvor, Alain Pelletier, Professor George Perlin, Dennis Pilon, Peter Puxley, and Professor John Trent.

Thanks also to Douglas Wands, Principal Officer of Scotland, The Electoral Commission; and Dr. Paul Harris, Chief Executive, Electoral Commission (New Zealand) for providing us with helpful information about the electoral systems in their respective countries. Thank you also to the Honourable Graham Kelly, High Commissioner of New Zealand for facilitating our discussions with representatives from New Zealand and for providing information about their electoral system. We also thank Mr. Paul Wilder, McDougall Trust and Professor Louis Massicotte, University of Montreal, for their valuable guidance on different aspects of the report. Thank you to Professor David Farrell, Department of Government, University of Manchester, for providing information about electoral system design, as well as comments and feedback on an earlier draft of this Report. Thank you also to Alasdair MacLeod, Editor Scottish Parliamentary Unit, BBC Scotland News and

Current Affairs for providing us with helpful information about election night media coverage in Scotland.

Over the course of this project, many members of the Advisory Council of the Law Commission have provided very helpful comments and feedback. Thank you to Sanjeev Anand, Jacques Auger, Darin Barney, Georges Berberi, Marie-Andrée Bertrand, June Callwood, Geneviève Cartier, Paul-André Comeau, Bradley Crawford, Ervan Cronk, Janet Dench, Margaret Denike, Irène d'Entremont, Wilma Derksen, Jean Dragon, Emerson Douyon, Leena Evic-Twerdin, Dave Farthing, Gerry A. Ferguson, Jean-Pierre Gariépy, Kenneth Hatt, Mavis Henry, Peggy Johnson, Andrée Lajoie, Heather McFadgen, Hans Mohr, Michael Morrison, Katherine Peterson, Alan Reynolds, Morris Rosenberg, Mary-Ellen Turpel-Lafond, and Jeff Wilbond.

Many commentators were asked to provide their comments and feedback on different drafts of this Report. We wish to thank Larry Gordon, Julian West, Darin Barney, Dennis Pilon, Dave Farthing, Rosemary Speirs, Gregory Tardy, and Manon Tremblay.

The Commission is particularly grateful to Professor Brian Tanguay who drafted the report and patiently incorporated the many suggestions that were made by the Commissioners. It was indeed a real pleasure to work with Professor Tanguay. We are very grateful for his rigorous research and elegant report drafting.

We are also grateful to Linda Larocque and her production and translation team for their very professional work.

The Commissioners also want to thank the employees at the Commission who worked to complete this Report. Several of the Commission's co-op and summer students contributed to finalizing the Report. Thank you to Jennifer Schmidt, Mélanie Mallet, Megan Celhoffer, Nicole Spencer, Éric Malo, Julie Alfesky, Kelly Ann Mahoney, Korinda MacLaine, and Drew Mildon. Other members of the team from the Commission to be thanked include Maryse St-Pierre, Jocelyne Geoffroy, Suzanne Schryer-Bélair, and Daniel Lanouette (administrative support), Lise Traversy and Stéphane Bachand (communications), and Lorraine Pelot and Karen Jensen (research). Bruno Bonneville, the former Executive Director, and his replacement Dennis Cooley supported the project throughout. Finally, our very special thanks to Steven Bittle, Senior Research Officer at the Commission, who wrote the Discussion Paper, and orchestrated the complete project, including the many facets of the research and consultation process, and finalized this Report. We owe him an enormous debt of gratitude.

Past Commissioners Alan Buchanan, Gwen Boniface, and Stephen Owen contributed to the early stages of this project. We thank them for their contributions.

The views expressed in this Report, along with any errors and omissions, are the responsibility of the Commissioners.

Executive Summary

Because elections play a central role in modern democracy, the particular formula employed to translate votes into seats in the legislature assumes special importance. Recently, some countries have questioned their electoral systems and the democratic values that they reflect, and have instituted reforms. Canada, for the most part, has been hesitant to experiment with its electoral system. However, a growing number of Canadians are interested in critically examining the existing electoral system, and many deem that it is time to change the way we cast our votes.

Beginning in 2001, the Law Commission of Canada conducted extended research and a multifaceted public consultation and engagement strategy to gather the insights and opinions of a broad cross section of Canadians on electoral system reform. This Report reflects many of the opinions and ideas that were expressed through this consultation process.

For the past decade or so, Canada has been in the grip of a democratic malaise evidenced by decreasing levels of political trust, declining voter turnout, increasing cynicism toward politicians and traditional forms of political participation, and growing disengagement of young people from politics. However, as the Commission heard throughout its consultation process, many citizens want to be involved, want to have a real voice in decision making, and would like to see more responsive, accountable, and effective political institutions.

While there is no single magic bullet that will instantaneously stimulate Canadians' involvement in the political system, a consensus appears to be emerging among political parties of all stripes, experts in electoral behaviour, and grassroots organizations that electoral system reform is a good starting point for energizing and strengthening Canadian democracy.

In this Report, the Commission attempts to answer several questions about electoral reform. Does our electoral system meet our democratic aspirations? Should we consider reforming the existing voting system? What alternatives could more accurately reflect the style of democratic governance that we prefer? Are these systems adaptable to the Canadian constitutional and political landscape? What should the reform process look like?

To stimulate reflection on and discussion of our system of democratic governance, this Report has several objectives:

- to understand the historical evolution of electoral reform debates in Canada and how arguments for reform have changed over time, and to understand the factors that help characterize contemporary discussion and debate;

- to assess the concerns about Canada's voting system, and to establish criteria for evaluating electoral systems;

- to explore the potential impact of electoral reform on our system of democratic governance;

- to make recommendations about electoral reform; and

- to explore how the process of electoral reform might unfold.

Families of Electoral Systems

One of the most common methods of classifying electoral systems is based on their proportionality, that is, how closely the number of seats in the legislature won by a party mirrors that party's share of the popular vote. Using this criterion, there are roughly nine types of electoral systems grouped into three families: plurality–majority systems, proportional representation systems, and semi-PR (proportional representation) systems. This Report examines the advantages and disadvantages, in a Canadian context, of these families and their nine offshoots.

Canada currently uses a plurality–majority system, which ensures that the winning candidate in a riding obtains at least a plurality of the votes cast. It is called a first-past-the-post system because, in some respects, it resembles horse races where the winner is the one who crosses the finish line first.

For many Canadians, this system is inherently unfair—more likely to frustrate or distort the wishes of the voters than to translate them fairly into representation and influence in the legislature. It has been criticized as:

- being overly generous to the party that wins a plurality of the vote, rewarding it with a legislative majority disproportionate to its share of the vote;

- allowing the governing party, with its artificially swollen legislative majority, to dominate the political agenda;

- promoting parties formed along regional lines, thus exacerbating Canada's regional divisions;

- leaving large areas of the country without adequate representatives in the governing party caucus;

- disregarding a large number of votes in that voters who do not vote for the winning candidate have no connection to the elected representative, nor to the eventual make-up of the House of Commons;

- contributing to the under-representation of women, minority groups, and Aboriginal peoples;

- preventing a diversity of ideas from entering the House of Commons; and

- favouring an adversarial style of politics.

Its shortcomings can be minimized by adding an element of proportionality to the electoral system—one that more accurately translates percentage of votes won into seats in the House of Commons.

Current Reform Proposals

Contemporary interest in electoral system reform in Canada has been motivated by new Canadian realities: a more mobile and diverse population, a declining voter turnout, decreasing youth participation, and recent election results.

For an increasing number of Canadians, the imbalances in our system of democracy are unacceptable. One of the driving forces for reform is the desire for a system that better reflects the country's diverse population and ideas. Another reason is found in the skewed results of recent provincial and federal elections, which many observers claim deny effective representation. Arguments for reform are also spurred by the belief that it may help improve voter turnout, which has been declining precipitously over the past decade. In the 2000 election, just over 61 percent of registered voters bothered to cast a ballot, the lowest figure for a federal election in Canadian history. Of particular concern is the lack of youth participation in traditional political processes. For example, only about 25 percent of eligible voters between the ages of 18 and 24 cast ballots in the 2000 federal general election.

International precedents have also moved electoral reform up the political agenda in the last decade or so. Included in this Report are lessons learned from the experiences of regions as diverse as New Zealand, Japan, Scotland, and Wales.

Democratic Values and the Choice of Electoral System

What criteria should we use to judge our current voting system? What criteria should we adopt to choose between different electoral systems? How do we determine which system is "better"?

Building on the examples from other countries, existing literature, as well as feedback and input received through its consultation process, the Commission chose ten criteria for assessing electoral systems:

- representation of parties;

- demographic representation;

- diverse ideas;

- geographic representation;

- effective government;

- accountable government;

- effective opposition;

- valuing votes;

- regional balance; and

- inclusive decision making.

Canada's first-past-the-post system performs poorly on many of these criteria. The Report examines some principal alternatives and improvements to the first-past-the-post electoral system, and assesses their relative strengths and weaknesses against the same criteria.

Electoral Options for Canada

In making its recommendations, the Commission's goal was to balance the benefits of introducing some element of proportionality into the existing system with the capacity to maintain accountable government, most notably as a direct link between elected politicians and their constituents. The Report, therefore, examines alternative systems from the premise that constituencies should stay small enough to maintain the Member of Parliament–constituent relationship. The Report also accepted the premise that there is little appetite for substantially increasing the size of the House of Commons to accommodate a new electoral system. Finally, the report is based on the premise that changes to the electoral system should be made without a process of constitutional amendment. These considerations, as well as our ten criteria, guided this exploration of eight different voting systems.

The conclusion of this survey is that adding an element of pro-portionality to Canada's electoral system, as inspired by the system currently used in Scotland, would be the most appropriate model for adoption. Its potential benefits include:

- reducing the discrepancy between a party's share of the seats in the House of Commons and its share of the votes;

- including in the House of Commons new and previously under-represented voices, such as smaller political parties;

- electing a greater number of minority group and women candidates;

- encouraging inter-party cooperation through coalition governments;

- reducing the huge disparities in the value of votes that currently exist, in which a vote for the winning party is often three to four times more "valuable" than a vote for any of the other parties;

- reducing the number of disregarded votes, thus increasing the number of "sincere," as opposed to strategic, votes; and

- producing more regionally balanced party caucuses.

The Commission, therefore, recommends adding an element of proportionality to Canada's electoral system, and that Canada adopt a mixed member proportional electoral system.

Implications of Adding an Element of Proportionality into Canada's Electoral System

This Report also considers the implications of introducing an element of proportionality into the current electoral system. Of particular interest are the impacts of minority or coalition governments on political decision making, questions about regionalism, the creation of two "classes" of representatives, issues of accountability, and the administrative costs of such an electoral system. The Report contains recommendations for dealing with several of these issues.

The Process of Electoral Reform—Engaging Citizens in Democratic Change

Finally, the Report explores how electoral reform fits within overall concerns about Canada's system of democratic governance. After all, we need to remember that democracy is more than just voting in a municipal, provincial, or federal election. Democracy is also about what happens between elections, how politicians and the electorate relate to each other, and the role that citizens play in their system of democratic governance.

How might the process of reform unfold? Drawing on the results of its consultation process, and the experiences of other Canadian jurisdictions, as well as the experiences of other countries, the Report concludes that it is crucial that citizens be included in an ongoing dialogue about electoral reform, and that the process of reform include a citizens' engagement strategy. Many Canadians are eager to participate in democratic governance, and they need and want information. This strategy should have diverse and broad representation, including representation from women, youth, minority groups, and all regions. It should seek the views of political parties (minority parties as well as mainstream parties), Parliamentarians, and citizens' groups. Any reform process should also include provision for formal review after implementing changes.

Conclusion

Canada inherited its first-past-the-post electoral system from Great Britain over 200 years ago, at a time when significant sections of the Canadian population, including women, Aboriginal people, and non-property owners, were disenfranchised. Throughout the first half of the 19th century and for 50 years after Confederation, the strengths of our electoral system were evident: it fostered competition between two major parties and provided the successful party with a strong, albeit artificial, legislative majority. Territory, embodied in the direct link between the Member of Parliament and his (for they were all men) constituents, was the most important aspect of a citizen's political identity and the pre-eminent feature of prevailing notions of representation.

Canada's political, cultural, and economic reality has vastly changed; the current electoral system no longer responds to 21st century Canadian democratic values. Many Canadians desire an electoral system that better reflects the society in which they live—one that includes a broader diversity of ideas and is more representative of

Canadian society. For these reasons, the Commission recommends adding an element of proportionality to our electoral system.

Furthermore, because of its many potential benefits, electoral reform should be a priority item on the political agenda. Overall, the Report recognizes that no single measure will suffice to address the complex challenges facing Canadian democracy in the 21st century. However, it has become apparent that the first-past-the-post electoral system no longer meets the democratic aspirations of many Canadians. Electoral reform is thus a necessary step to energize and strengthen Canadian democracy.

Chapter 1 Introduction

1.1 Canada's Electoral System

Elections are a cornerstone of our modern democracy. Healthy political systems should allow voters to engage in an ongoing dialogue with government decision makers, informing them of the policies and programs that they deem essential and rendering judgment on the effectiveness or desirability of the government's decisions. Regular and fair elections, conducted in a political climate that encourages the free exchange of ideas and opinions, are a crucial element of the relationship between citizens and their government.

Because elections play a central role in modern democracy, the particular formula employed to translate votes into seats in the legislature assumes special importance. There are numerous varieties of electoral formulas currently in use in the world, and many more that have been experimented with or proposed in the past. Each system reflects a range of values that not only help to determine how political candidates will be elected to a legislature, but also contribute to a country's culture of governance. For example, a system might encourage the representation of different currents of public opinion, or the election of representatives from diverse groups—social, cultural, religious, and so on. Alternatively, a system may be geared toward producing majority governments where a single political party dominates the policy agenda for a period of time. In other instances, a system may attempt to balance the value of majority governments with the goal of encouraging the broad representation of different groups and political ideas. Each electoral system attempts to balance as many different democratic values as is desirable, but there are necessarily trade-offs among them.

From time to time, citizens reflect upon the "fit" between their electoral system and their prevailing democratic values. In recent years, some countries have engaged in reflection and critique, raising questions about their electoral systems and possible reforms. Canada, for the most part, has been hesitant to experiment with its electoral system.[1] Despite this, however, there are several factors that highlight the increasing importance of including electoral reform on the democratic reform agenda, as well as signs that a growing number of Canadians are interested in critically examining the existing electoral system. In recent years, throughout the country, citizens' groups, academics, politicians, and political parties have been arguing that it is time to change the way in which we cast our votes in provincial, territorial, and federal elections.

In this Report, the Commission attempts to answer several questions about reforming Canada's first-past-the-post (FPTP) electoral system: Does this electoral system continue to meet Canadians' democratic aspirations? Should Canadians consider reforming the existing voting system? How should we go about deciding whether it is time for change? What alternatives exist that could more accurately reflect the style of democratic governance that Canadians desire? Are these systems adaptable to the Canadian constitutional and political landscape? What should the reform process look like? These questions invite us to reflect seriously upon our system of democratic governance and to measure its successes and shortcomings.

Canada's electoral system is a single-member plurality system, most commonly known as the first-past-the-post system. Candidates are elected to the House of Commons through elections in one of 301 ridings (308 after the forthcoming electoral boundaries redistribution). One member from each riding is elected by a plurality of the votes (not necessarily a majority, or more than 50 percent of the votes)—the winner simply needs to have more votes than his or her opponents. The party that forms the government is generally the party that is able to see the largest number of its candidates elected in the 301 ridings, regardless of its overall share of the popular vote in the country. A party can win a majority of seats in the legislature with less than 50 percent of the vote.

1.2 Democratic Reform and Electoral Systems

As we progress into the 21st century, a growing number of Canadians have expressed their desire for more meaningful relationships with various levels of government, and a greater voice in decision-making processes. Canada, like many of the developed nations of the West, has for the past decade or so been in the grip of a democratic malaise. Its symptoms include, among other things, declining levels of political trust, declining voter turnout, increasing cynicism and hostility toward politicians and traditional forms of political participation (such as political parties) and growing disengagement of young people from politics. There is considerable evidence to suggest that these changing political sensibilities may be symptomatic of a longer-term shift in citizens' attitudes toward politics.[2] Increasingly, citizens in advanced democracies are unwilling to accept a passive role in the political system. As the Commission has heard throughout its consultation process, many citizens want to be involved, have a real voice in decision making, and would like to see more responsive, accountable, and effective political institutions. Many perceive the mainstream mechanisms of politics—parties, legislatures, bureaucracies—to be insufficiently inclusive or responsive.

There have been a number of investigations of the causes of this democratic malaise or democratic deficit, a term that refers to the disparity in power and influence between political decision makers, on the one hand, and citizens, on the other.[3] The expression refers to both broad systemic issues, such as a perceived political disempowerment related to globalization, as well as concerns with different aspects of the political system, including electoral reform, excessive party discipline, the erosion of influence of individual Members of Parliament, or the overwhelming influence of the executive (the Prime Minister and the Prime Minister's Office), and overly adversarial politics in the House of Commons.[4]

In Quebec, for example, the notion of a democratic deficit is a consistent theme throughout the report of Quebec's Estates-General on the Reform of Democratic Institutions (prepared by the Béland Commission, named after its chairperson, Claude Béland). In 2002, the Béland Commission held 27 public forums in every region of the

> "… looking at each of the past two general elections, the number of people who did not vote at all was larger than the number of people who voted for the winning party. Now, we can rationalize these results with reference to political circumstances or social change, but at some stage we have to face up to the fact: something is going wrong here, and in a fundamental way. Casting a ballot is the most basic function of our democratic system. That so many Canadians chose not to do so is the political equivalent of the canary in the coalmine. It demonstrates graphically how high the stakes surrounding reform are—that far too many Canadians cannot be bothered to vote because they don't think their vote matters."
>
> P. Martin, "The Democratic Deficit" (December 2002–January 2003) 24: 1 *Policy Options* at 11.

province and met with more than 2,000 citizens. Throughout these consultations many citizens complained about the distortion in election results and that most existing democratic institutions lack real power, that power seems to be centralized in the hands of the executive, that excessive party discipline weakens the role of elected representatives, and that women, ethnic minorities, and Aboriginal people continue to be under-represented in the legislature and other government organizations.[5] In concrete terms, citizens in Quebec above all demand "that the rules governing the exercise of democracy in Quebec be changed so that Quebecers can get closer to legislative power if they so desire and, collectively, be more effective in exercising some control over it." [Translation][6]

Given the nature and extent of voter unhappiness with many of Canada's existing democratic institutions, it is clear that there is no single magic bullet that will instantaneously stimulate Canadians' involvement in the political system. At the same time, however, there appears to be an emerging consensus among political parties of all stripes, experts in electoral behaviour, and grassroots organizations that an important starting point is electoral system reform.[7]

> "The heart of our citizenry, if one may so speak, is deeply troubled. Across the province, Quebecers are extremely disillusioned with politics. Their frustration with their powerlessness to influence decisions that affect their lives and those of their fellow citizens is palpable. One major source of disappointment is the voting sytem; citizens do not feel that their vote is truly and systematically reflected in the composition of the National Assembly." [Translation]
>
> —Quebec, Steering Committee of the Estates-General on the Reform of Democratic Institutions, *Prenez votre place! La participation citoyenne au cœur des institutions démocratiques québécoises* (Quebec, March 2003) at 21.

Recent trends in provincial politics illuminate an increased willingness on the part of many Canadians to question the existing electoral system. Governments in many provinces—such as British Columbia, Ontario, Quebec, New Brunswick, and Prince Edward Island—have initiated democratic review processes that include examinations of the electoral system. These initiatives are joined by a chorus of voices in civil society that argue it is time to engage Canadians in serious discussion and debate about the merits of the existing voting system and its alternatives. In addition to the Commission's research and consultation process, organizations such as the Institute for Research on Public Policy have facilitated research and dialogue on electoral system reform; many academics and journalists continue to debate the issues; and a number of grassroots organizations, for example, Equal Voice, Fair Vote Canada, Democracy Watch, Mouvement pour une démocratie nouvelle, Fair Voting B.C., and Every Vote Counts in Prince Edward Island, are actively raising awareness about the need for electoral system reform in Canada.

In many respects, recent concerns with Canada's first-past-the-post electoral system reflect a growing distaste with the characteristic results of this voting method. For example, Howe and Northrup, using data from a 2000 survey conducted for the Institute for Research on Public Policy, and from a 1990 poll done for the Royal Commission on

Electoral Reform and Party Financing, conclude that a majority of voters believe that the first-past-the-post electoral system is unfair or unacceptable.[8] Figure 1, adapted from the Howe and Northrup study, shows that Canadians in 2000 were more likely to be critical of the first-past-the-post system than they had been in 1990. In 1990, 39 percent found this system unacceptable; ten years later, 49 percent found it unacceptable. The authors also noted that there were important regional variations in these attitudes, with voters in British Columbia the most critical of the first-past-the-post system in 2000 (63 percent found voting results under it to be "unacceptable"), followed by those in Quebec (51 percent negative).

Figure 1 Voters' opinions on first-past-the-post election results, 1990 and 2000

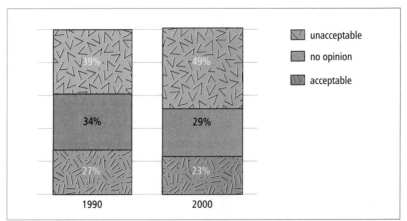

Adapted from P. Howe and D. Northrup "Strengthening Canadian Democracy: The Views of Canadians" (2000) 1:5 *Policy Matters* at 14.

For Howe and Northrup, the "seeming decrease in support for the current electoral system indicates the importance of initiating public debate on the strengths and weaknesses of both first-past-the-post and alternative electoral systems."[9]

"Ontario's recent election campaign was as hard-fought, adversarial and personal as they come. The policy platforms and leadership styles of the three main contenders were starkly different. The stakes for the province had rarely been higher. You might think, therefore, that voter turnout on Oct. 2 would have been unusually heavy. And you might think that Liberal Leader Dalton McGuinty's sweeping victory—72 seats, compared with 24 for the Tories and seven for the New Democrats—would have marked a triumph for representative democracy. But you would be wrong.

Although the Ontario premier-designate's big win did reaffirm the people's capacity to 'throw the rascals out,' it was nowhere near as decisive as the final seat tally suggests. The Liberals won only 46 per cent of the popular vote, less than a clear majority. And fewer than half of Mr. McGuinty's MPPs garnered more than 50-per cent support in their ridings.

His 'landslide' was really a function of Ontario's winner-take-all, first-past-the-post electoral system. And kitten-eater controversy notwithstanding, voter turnout was only 57 per cent. Forty-three per cent of eligible Ontario voters, more than enough to have decisively changed the outcome, didn't even bother to show up.

Why did so many neglect to vote? Perhaps for the same reason that kept 40 per cent of eligible Canadians on the sidelines in the 2000 federal election. In 1997, Prime Minister Jean Chretien's Liberals had won only 39 per cent of the popular vote. But because of vote-splitting between the Canadian Alliance and Progressive Conservatives, and the winner-take-all system, Mr. Chretien won a second majority. Sixty-one per cent of the electorate had chosen parties other than his.

Small wonder many felt disenfranchised and opted out next time around. It's the same dynamic that tends to make liberal-leaning federal voters apathetic in Alberta, where the Alliance has a perpetual stranglehold.

A growing number of Canadians, from every region and every hue of the political spectrum, are unhappy with this state of affairs. They feel alienated from the political process. Many want electoral reform ..."

The Globe and Mail, "Suppose the outcome reflected all the votes."
(16 October 2003) (Editorial) at A26.
Reprinted with permission from *The Globe and Mail*.

> "If we are to explore the alternatives to the current FPTP system, as we should, we must do so carefully, soberly, and with a realistic understanding of the limits of electoral engineering. Regional alienation, Quebec *souverainisme*, discrimination against women and minorities, flawed political parties—these problems cannot be eliminated by a new electoral system. But as we reconsider the institutional arrangements inherited from Britain over 130 years ago, we have to ask whether so many of our citizens should continue to 'waste' their votes, and whether the very survival of a major political organization (such as the federal PC and New Democratic parties) should depend on the caprices of an arbitrary and unpredictable electoral system. We can, and should, do better."
>
> H. MacIvor, "A Brief Introduction to Electoral Reform," in Henry Milner, ed., *Making Every Vote Count* (Peterborough: Broadview Press, 1999) at 34.

1.3 Concerns with the Status Quo

What are the limits of Canada's electoral system? Why are some federal parties, grassroots organizations, and a growing number of Canadians interested in electoral reform? Why do an increasing number of Canadians believe that the current electoral system no longer fits with Canadian democratic values?

For many Canadians, our system is inherently unfair—more likely to frustrate or distort the wishes of the voters than to translate them fairly into representation and influence in the legislature. Specifically, critics put forth the following arguments.[10]

- The first-past-the-post system is overly generous to the party that wins a plurality of the vote in a general election, rewarding it with a legislative majority that is disproportionate to its share of the vote. For example, in a riding with three or four candidates (something that is common in Canada), a candidate could be elected with 34 percent of the votes. In turn, a party can form a majority government despite having received less than 50 percent of the votes.

- It allows the governing party, with its artificially swollen legislative majority, to dominate the political agenda almost completely for a period of four or five years, thereby contributing to the weakening of Parliament. In cases where a party holds a majority of the seats in the legislature after receiving a minority of the popular vote, opposition parties that received a significant proportion of the vote are relatively powerless in participating in or challenging the governing party's policy agenda.

This "tendency of the plurality system to misrepresent the outcome of the popular vote, and its ability to wipe out entire parties (and oppositions) that have substantial electoral support, raises questions about the democratic legitimacy of the system."

J.A. Cousins, *Electoral Reform for Prince Edward Island: A Discussion Paper*. (Charlottetown: Institute of Island Studies at the University of Prince Edward Island, 2000), online: <http://www.upei.ca/islandstudies/rep_jac_2.htm> (date accessed: 19 December 2003).

- It promotes parties formed along regional lines, thus exacerbating Canada's regional divisions, and conversely penalizes parties with diffuse national support. Many argue that, under the first-past-the-post system, parties are encouraged to focus their efforts on regions of the country where they are most likely to win a plurality of the votes. At the same time, parties with diffuse national support but no regional stronghold might have difficulty winning in enough ridings to gain representation in the House of Commons.

- It can leave large areas of the country without adequate representatives in the governing party caucus. Due to the regional nature of the first-past-the-post system, the ruling party's success is often attributable to winning a large percentage of seats in particular regions of the country. Many observers express concern about the fact that the ruling party may have few or no caucus members from certain parts of the country.

- This system disregards a large number of votes: unless a voter supports the winning candidate in a given riding, there is no connection between the voter's choice and the eventual make-up of the House of Commons. Many critics suggest that this aspect of the electoral system discourages people from voting since it leaves them with the impression that their vote does not matter.

- It contributes to the under-representation of women, minority groups, and Aboriginal peoples. Critics maintain that countries with first-past-the-post systems routinely under-represent women and minority candidates. Neither women nor minority candidates are regionally concentrated and, therefore, cannot benefit from regional concentration. As well, in the first-past-the-post "winner takes all" system, parties attempt to maximize their chances of success by running the "safest" candidates possible, that is, candidates that the party believes will win a plurality of the vote. Therefore, women and minority candidates are not readily nominated.

- It prevents diversity within the House of Commons. As a result of regional concentration, disproportionate votes to seats, and an under-representation of women and minority candidates, legislatures within this system lack a diversity of voices in political decision-making processes.

- This system favours an adversarial style of politics. Critics suggest that parties that do not win the majority of seats in the legislature or House of Commons are left with few options but to attack and criticize other parties' policy positions, thereby contributing to a culture of adversarial politics.

"I personally believe the present electoral system exaggerates regional tensions ... [O]ne of my frustrations is that the rest of Canada stereotypes Alberta as Alliance country because of the number of seats the party has here. But a look at the official voting results shows that though in 1997 the Alliance received 24 of 26 seats, it received only 54.6% of the vote. In 2000 the results got only marginally fairer with the Alliance receiving 23 of the 26 seats based on 58.9% of the vote ... The regional imbalance in representation isn't just a matter of perception. It means the government and opposition caucuses are regionally imbalanced. The current government caucus is about 60% Ontarian, while the official opposition caucus is 75% from BC and Alberta. The first-past-the-post electoral system also made the Bloc [Québécois] the official opposition in the mid-90s.

The West is not just right wing. Not all Quebecers want to separate. Every citizen who lives in Ontario is not a Liberal and it isn't only Atlantic Canada that supports the Progressive Conservatives or the NDP [New Democratic Party]. But our present voting system certainly suggests that this is true. If these perceptions were harmless, I would have no quibble. But these myths have lives of their own and destructively influence Canadians' perceptions of each other.

I want an electoral system that more accurately reflects the percentage of votes a party receives. Because of the size of Canada, my personal preference is for a system which combines geographical representation with proportional voting. But this preference is not fixed in stone. My bottom line is an electoral system that more fairly reflects Canadians' voting preferences."

Harvey Voogd, Edmonton, Alberta. Feedback from Law Commission of Canada's consultation process. (Received: 6 May 2003.)

This is not to deny, however, that the first-past-the-post system has its supporters, who present arguments in its favour.

- The system is easily understood by the average voter. At election time, voters simply mark the ballot (with a cross or other mark) beside the name of their preferred candidate.[11]

- It can produce majority governments that take decisive action.

- This system allows voters to oust an unpopular government at the next election.

- It creates a clear geographic link between Members of Parliament and constituents.

A growing number of Canadians believe that the strengths of the first-past-the-post system may come at too great a cost—that it's "too much of a good thing"—by allowing governments with "artificial" majorities to misrepresent the views of the Canadian public. In short, they argue that the drawbacks of our electoral system may outweigh its advantages. In this Report, we review arguments for and against this system, and consider whether some changes could minimize its shortcomings. For many, adding an element of proportionality to the electoral system—one which more accurately translates percentage of votes won into seats in the legislature or House of Commons— would help in addressing the many drawbacks of this system.

> "The Canadian political record was for long an impressive one, but it has not recently produced much stability … or successful national unity. While it would be wrong to attribute the Quebec problem to FPTP [first-past-the-post], it would also be wrong to say that Canadian experience provides evidence for FPTP being a nationally unifying system."
>
> United Kingdom, Independent Commission on the Voting System, Final Report, (1988) at para. 77.

1.4 Objectives and Organization of this Report

This Report is part of a process of asking questions, stimulating debate, and making recommendations relating to Canada's system of democratic governance. It reviews the validity and strength of arguments for and against reforming Canada's voting system, while also examining different systems and considering the potential impacts of electoral reform on the country's system of governance. This Report seeks ways to help energize and strengthen Canadian democracy.

The first objective of this Report is to understand the historical evolution of electoral reform debates in Canada in order to understand how the arguments for reform have changed over time, and to understand the factors that help characterize contemporary discussion and debate about Canada's electoral system. The first part of Chapter 2 provides an overview of the different families of electoral systems that are used throughout the world. Chapter 2 then briefly examines some of Canada's past electoral reform efforts from the late 19th and early 20th centuries to attempts in the late 1970s to introduce some element of proportionality into Canada's voting system. It also takes a closer look at the confluence of several social issues and trends that have propelled the electoral reform debate onto the political agenda in many parts of the country.

The second objective is to explore the validity of growing concerns with Canada's voting system. To this end, the Report discusses the values that Canadians would like to see reflected in their system of democratic governance. Chapter 3 establishes a set of ten criteria for examining electoral systems, including criteria such as representation of parties, demographic representation, inclusive decision making, and valuing votes, among others. At the same time, we note that the first-past-the-post system fosters close identification between constituents and a single representative. We conclude by suggesting that it is possible to introduce corrective elements to our existing electoral system to alleviate some of its shortcomings. In particular, we propose that changes be made to the electoral system to accommodate an element of proportionality.

The third objective is to make recommendations for electoral reform in Canada. Chapter 4 offers recommendations for introducing an element of proportionality into the voting system, including how to address some of the common criticisms that are levied against proportional representation. The Law Commission's work in this and subsequent chapters is based on a constitutional analysis that ensures the recommendations are viable within the country's existing constitutional framework.

The fourth objective is to explore the potential impact of electoral reform on Canada's system of democratic governance. Chapter 5 considers several implications of introducing an element of proportionality into the current electoral system. Of particular interest are the impacts of minority or coalition governments on political decision making, questions about regionalism, two "classes" of representatives under proportional systems, issues of accountability, and the administrative costs of such an electoral system. Chapter 5 offers recommendations relating to these issues.

The final objective of the Report is to explore how the process of electoral reform might unfold. Chapter 6 explores how we might move to remedy some shortcomings of the first-past-the-post system

"When we speak of [democratic] goals to be achieved, there should be no illusion that the electoral system can, by itself, achieve them. Electoral systems shape and constrain the way in which politicians and constituents behave, but they are only one small part of the forces affecting the total constellation of behaviour, even of political behaviour. Miracles do not follow from changes of electoral systems. No one should expect more than incremental changes in behavioural patterns once the configuration of electoral incentives is altered. *But sometimes increments of change can be surpassingly important.*"

D.L. Horowitz, "Electoral Systems: A Primer For Decision Makers" (2003) 14: 4 *Journal of Democracy* at 116. (Emphasis added.)

in a way that allows citizens to participate in the reform process. It also looks at how electoral reform fits within overall concerns about Canada's system of democratic governance. In this respect, Chapter 6 reminds us that democracy is more than just the process of voting in a municipal, provincial, or federal election. Democracy is also about what happens between elections, how politicians and the electorate relate to each other, and the role that citizens play in their system of democratic governance.

Overall, the Report recognizes that no single measure will suffice to address the complex challenges facing Canadian democracy in the 21st century. However, it has become apparent that the first-past-the-post electoral system no longer meets the democratic aspirations of many Canadians. Electoral reform is thus a necessary first step to energize and strengthen Canadian democracy.

---

1   A. Lijphart, *Electoral Systems and Party Systems: A Study of Twenty-Seven Democracies, 1945–1990* (Oxford: Oxford University Press, 1994) at 53.

2   See, for example, P. Howe and D. Northrup, "Strengthening Canadian Democracy: The Views of Canadians" (2000) 1:5 *Policy Matters*, Centre for Canadian Studies at Mount Allison University, *The Canada Democratic Audit*, online: <http://www.mta.ca/faculty/arts-letters/canadian_studies/audit.htm> (date accessed: 30 November 2003).

3   The notion of a "democratic deficit" became popular in Western Europe in the 1980s and early 1990s as the drive for a unified Europe gathered momentum. Euroskeptics worried that decision-making authority was leaching away from national governments to the technocrats in Brussels, and in particular to the secretive and powerful European Commission. For further discussion, see D. Dinan, *Ever Closer Union? An Introduction to the European Community* (Boulder: Lynne Reiner Publishers, 1994). In everyday Canadian parlance, the term "democratic deficit" is used metaphorically to describe the gap between prime ministerial power on the one hand and a weakened Parliament on the other, or between what might be called the political or elite class and ordinary citizens.

4   Centre for Canadian Studies at Mount Allison University, *supra* note 2.

5   Quebec, Steering Committee of the Estates-General on the Reform of Democratic Institutions, *Prenez Votre Place! La participation citoyenne au coeur des institutions démocratiques québécoises* (2003) at 22–23.

6   *Ibid.* at 25.

7   According to Seidle, "[p]ublic opinion is not driving the debate on electoral reform, although there is evidence that Canadians might support it … Although electoral system reform [in Canada] does not have a high level of salience in public opinion … it is fair to say that a policy community … has emerged. This policy community consists of scholars, research organizations like the Institute for Research on Public Policy (IRPP), certain federal and provincial political parties, and a number of grassroots organizations like Fair Vote Canada, all of which aim to move the topic of electoral system reform closer to the center of public debate." F.L. Seidle, *Electoral System Reform in Canada: Objectives, Advocacy and Implications for Governance* (Ottawa: Canadian Policy Research Networks Inc., 2002) at xiii.

8   Howe and Northrup, *supra* note 2 at 13–16. Voters were asked: "Under the present election system, a party can win a majority of the seats and form the government without winning a majority of the votes; do you find this acceptable or unacceptable, or do you not have an opinion on this?" In a variation of the question for the 2000 survey, voters were asked whether they found this to be "fair" or "unfair." The use of the terms "fair" and "unfair" lowered the number of respondents who had no opinion on the issue, and increased the proportion who were critical of first-past-the-post by about 5 percentage points. The Institute for Research on Public Policy sample size was 1,278, while the Royal Commission on Electoral Reform and Party Financing sample size was 2,947.

9   Howe and Northrup, *supra* note 2 at 15. Seidle, *supra* note 7 at 13, injects a cautionary note on this subject, observing that there is widespread misunderstanding of existing electoral rules among voters, and that "any process of citizen engagement on this issue must also address the need for public education." Seidle cites a study conducted by IPSOS-Reid in February 2001, which interviewed respondents on their attitudes toward—and knowledge of—the electoral system. The study found, among other things, that a significant number of Canadians do not understand FPTP. "Fully 50 per cent of our respondents believe that a candidate must get a majority of all votes cast in a riding in order to win a Parliamentary seat. And 47 per cent believe that a political party must win a majority of all votes cast in order to form a government." See, D. Bricker and M. Redfern, "Canadian Perspectives on the Voting System" (2001) 22:6 *Policy Options* at 22.

10 Most of these criticisms about the first-past-the-post system are taken, with slight modifications and additions, from B. Schwartz and D. Rettie, *Valuing Canadians: The Options for Voting System Reform in Canada* (Ottawa: Law Commission of Canada, 2002).

11 It should be noted that voters in many countries are quite capable of understanding fairly complex electoral systems, such as single transferable vote and various types of mixed systems.

Chapter 2 Reviewing Electoral Systems and Reform Proposals in Canada

2.1 Introduction

Chapter 2 describes different types of electoral systems currently in use around the world, classifying them according to the formulas they use to translate votes into seats in legislatures. Section 2.3 takes a closer look at the historical evolution of electoral reform in Canada mentioning some of the factors that have propelled concerns with the electoral system onto the political agenda in recent years.

2.2 Families of Electoral Systems

One of the most common methods of classifying electoral systems is based on their *proportionality*, that is, how closely the number of seats in the legislature won by a party mirrors that party's share of the popular vote. Using these criteria, there are roughly nine types of electoral systems, which in turn can be grouped into three broad families.[1]

Figure 2 depicts these families of electoral systems. Although each system employs its own unique ways of translating votes into seats, it is important to note that there are many variations within particular families, and that there are some commonalities and overlap between systems from different families. The broken line in figure 2 around the boxes representing mixed member proportional and mixed member majoritarian (two systems that we believe have particular relevance for Canada, as discussed in Chapter 4) underscores the fact that both systems use elements of proportional and plurality–majority voting.

2.2.1 Plurality–Majority Systems

A plurality–majority system is currently used for federal, provincial, and territorial elections in Canada. Plurality–majority systems ensure that

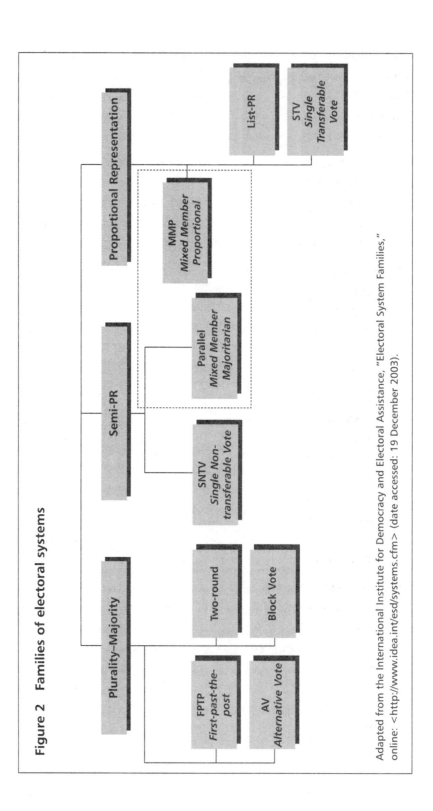

Figure 2 Families of electoral systems

Adapted from the International Institute for Democracy and Electoral Assistance, "Electoral System Families," online: <http://www.idea.int/esd/systems.cfm> (date accessed: 19 December 2003).

the winning candidate in a riding obtains at least a plurality of the votes cast, making the election similar, in some respects, to a horse race in that the winner is the one who crosses the finish line first. These systems are considered the least proportional types of electoral systems.[2] There are four basic types of plurality–majority systems.

- **First-past-the-post System:** Also known as the single-member plurality system, this system is currently used in Canada, the United Kingdom, the United States, and India, along with a number of countries historically influenced by Great Britain, such as Jamaica, Bahamas, and Saint Kitts and Nevis.

- **Alternative Vote System:** In this type of system, contests are held in single-member constituencies, but voters rank order candidates. If no candidate receives a majority of the votes, the lowest ranked candidate is dropped and his or her second preferences are then re-distributed among the remaining candidates. This process continues until a candidate with a majority (more than 50 percent) of the preferences emerges.

- **Block Vote System:** This is first-past-the-post in multi-member constituencies. Voters can cast as many votes as there are candidates. For example, if there are 10 seats to be filled in a constituency with 20 candidates, then voters will vote for as many candidates as they want, and the 10 candidates who receive the most votes win seats in the legislature. This system is currently used in the Palestinian Authority, Bermuda, and the Philippines, among other countries.

- **Two-round System:** This is also known as a run-off system, since two elections are held in single-member constituencies, usually a week or two apart. Any candidate winning a majority of the vote (more than 50 percent) in the first round is declared the winner. If no candidate receives a majority in a riding, then a second round of balloting is held, with only the top two candidates proceeding, and the winner of this round is declared elected. This system is used, most notably, in France.

2.2.2 Proportional Representation Systems

As the name suggests, proportional representational systems are the most proportional types of electoral systems. Proportional representation includes three basic types of systems.

- **List-PR System:** Each party "presents a list of candidates to the electorate, voters vote for a party, and parties receive seats in proportion to their overall share of the national vote. Winning candidates are taken from the lists in order of their position on the lists."[3] Most of the European democracies employ a list-PR system.

- **Single Transferable Vote System:** This system employs the alternative vote in multi-member districts. It allows the voter to rank order candidates. Typically, voters may either vote for only one candidate or rank as many as they wish (up to the number to be elected in the riding). Candidates from the same party may compete against each other in the same riding. A "quota" is established and any candidate who wins more votes than this quota is declared elected.[4] The "surplus votes" of these candidates—those in excess of the quota—are redistributed to second preferences of the voters who voted for these candidates. If there are still seats to be filled, then the candidate ranked last is eliminated and the second preferences of the voters who had voted for him or her are redistributed. This process is repeated until all of the riding seats are filled. The International Institute for Democracy and Electoral Assistance labels this "the most sophisticated of all electoral systems, allowing for choice between parties and between candidates within parties. The final results also retain a fair degree of proportionality …"[5] It has been used in Ireland and Malta, as well as for elections to the Australian Senate and to Tasmania's lower house.

- **Mixed Member Proportional System:** Many countries and regions have adopted this system, including Germany, Scotland, Wales, New Zealand, Bolivia, Hungary, and Venezuela. A proportion of representatives in these countries, usually between 50 percent and 60 percent, are elected from single-member constituencies using the first-past-the-post method, while the remainder are elected from party lists on the basis of a party's share of the popular vote. Voters have two votes, one for their constituency representative and one for the party. Figure 3 illustrates a mock ballot from a mixed member proportional electoral system.

Figure 3   Mixed member proportional system

You have two votes	
Party Vote	**Local Candidate Vote**
This vote decides the share of seats which each of the parties listed below will have in Parliament. Vote by putting a tick in the box next to the party you choose.	This vote decides the candidate who will be elected Member of Parliament for the Seashore riding. Vote by putting a tick in the box next to the candidate you wish to choose.
Vote for only one party	**Vote for only one candidate**
Red Party ❑ Blue Party ❑ White Party ❑ Green Party ❑	Candidate A ❑ Red Party Candidate B ❑ Blue Party Candidate C ❑ White Party Candidate D ❑ Green Party

This mock ballot is adapted from Elections New Zealand, "New Zealand's Electoral System: How Parliament is Elected," online: <http://www.elections.org.nz/elections/esyst/govt_elect.html> (date accessed: 5 January 2004). The candidate and party names have been changed to reflect the examples used in this Report.

The Party Vote portion of the ballot in figure 3 determines the proportion of seats in the legislature to which each party is entitled. The Local Candidate Vote portion is determined by the first-past-the-post method. To give a very simple example: if the country that uses this ballot has a 100-seat legislature (50 constituencies for local candidates plus 50 proportional representation seats), and the Red Party obtains 42 percent of the party vote, then it is entitled to 42 seats in the legislature. If the Red Party wins 30 of the seats for local candidates, then it is allotted 12 list seats to make up the difference.[6] In most countries using mixed member proportional systems, these lists are closed, that is, the parties draw them up before the election and voters are not allowed to alter the ranking of candidates.[7] The distinguishing feature that separates these from semi-PR, or "parallel" systems is that the number of seats a party takes from its list is partly determined by the number of seats it wins in the constituency races.[8] The overall results in these systems are highly proportional, that is, for each party, the percentage of seats it obtains in the legislature closely mirrors its share of the vote.

2.2.3 Semi-PR Systems

Semi-PR systems are an intermediate family of electoral systems that combine features of proportional representation with majority–plurality voting. Of the 211 countries surveyed by the International Institute for Democracy and Electoral Assistance in 1997, 22 (10 percent) have adopted a form of semi-PR system. There are two basic types.

- **Single Non-transferable Vote System:** Each voter has only one vote, but there are multiple candidates elected in the riding. Candidates with the highest vote totals win the seats.[9] For example, imagine a riding with 100 voters in which four candidates are to be elected. Four parties present as many candidates as they wish. In this instance, the results are as follows: Candidate A of the Red Party wins 40 votes; Candidate B also of the Red Party wins 40 votes; Candidate C of the Green Party wins 8 votes; Candidate D of the White Party wins 4 votes; Candidate E of the Red Party wins 3 votes; Candidate F of the Green Party wins 2 votes; Candidate G of the Blue Party wins

2 votes; and Candidate H of the Blue Party obtains a single vote. Candidates A, B, C, and D are elected, the last with only 4 percent of the popular vote. Table 1 illustrates the election results from this fictitious riding.

Table 1   Election results using a single non-transferable
          vote system

Candidate Name and Party	Percent of Votes Received (100 Voters)	Elected or Not Elected
Candidate A Red Party	40	Yes
Candidate B Red Party	40	Yes
Candidate C Green Party	8	Yes
Candidate D White Party	4	Yes
Candidate E Red Party	3	No
Candidate F Green Party	2	No
Candidate G Blue	2	No
Candidate H Blue Party	1	No

The greatest drawback of this system is its tendency toward factionalism and internal party politics, as candidates from the same party running in the same riding attempt to outspend each other to win a seat.[10] This system is currently used in Jordan, and was used to elect representatives to the Japanese Diet from 1948 to 1993.

• **Parallel or Mixed Member Majoritarian System:** This system is truly a hybrid or mixed system. Countries like Japan (since

1993), Russia, and South Korea have parallel or mixed member majoritarian systems: in each, a portion of the representatives are elected on the basis of some form of plurality–majority voting (usually first-past-the-post, but some countries employ two-round systems and block vote as well) and a portion on the basis of proportional representation. In Japan, for example, 60 percent of the representatives in the Diet are elected from single-member constituencies using first-past-the-post, while the remaining 40 percent are elected from party lists. Unlike mixed member proportional systems, the proportional representation compo-nent in these systems does not compensate for disproportionate results in the constituency elections; the two components of the system act independently or parallel to each other.[11]

2.3 Electoral Reform in Canada[12]

Electoral system reform in Canada is not without historical precedent. For more than 130 years, Canada's first-past-the-post voting system has been a source of discussion and debate, particularly following highly disproportionate election results.[13] In addition, significant reforms occurred in different parts of the country and throughout Canada's history. This section explores the history of electoral system reform in Canada.

2.3.1 Early Reform Efforts

Beginning in the late 19th and early 20th centuries, electoral system reform was sparked primarily by the extension of the franchise (the right to vote) to non-property owners and the working class, and to women, who had been previously excluded from voting. During this period, adopting some form of proportional representation was often one of the principal demands of newly-powerful social democratic parties.

Various progressive and united farmers' parties also helped encourage electoral reform in the wake of World War I, culminating in the adoption of proportional representation for municipal elections in all four western provinces. Manitoba and Alberta also adopted alternative voting systems (notably the single transferable vote for provincial elections in urban ridings) and the alternative vote in rural ridings. These systems were in place from the early 1920s until the mid-1950s, when they were replaced by first-past-the-post systems. In many instances, proportional representation systems were replaced in order to quell opposition parties that had begun to challenge ruling governments.[14]

Significant reform also occurred in 1916 when the provinces of Manitoba, Alberta, and Saskatchewan extended the franchise to women for provincial elections. Other provinces followed, and in 1918, universal suffrage rights were granted to non-aboriginal women age 21 or over for federal elections. These reforms followed decades of struggle by women suffragists to extend the vote to women.[15] The first general election in Canada in which women voted occurred in 1921, which was also when Agnes Macphail became Canada's first woman elected to the House of Commons.[16]

> " ... voting reforms were touted whenever the [CCF] made an impressive showing in the polls, by-elections, or provincial contests."
>
> D. Pilon, "Renewing Canadian Democracy: Citizen Engagement in Voting System Reform" (Ottawa: Law Commission of Canada, 2002) at 116.

From the 1930s until just after the Second World War,[17] a social democratic party, the Cooperative Commonwealth Federation (CCF) appeared on the scene, rapidly becoming the official opposition in British Columbia, Saskatchewan, and Ontario. Some observers argue that the mainstream parties and the media began to consider the possibility of adopting some form of proportional voting system, fearing that the CCF might form a majority government in a number of provinces under the existing first-past-the-post system.[18] In the early 1950s, the governing Liberal–Conservative coalition in British Columbia adopted the alternative vote for the provincial election held in 1952, in the hope that the new ballot would allow voters to support the Liberal–Conservative alternative and thus prevent the CCF from taking power. As it turned out, the beneficiary of this electoral innovation was a new party, the Social Credit Party, which eventually reverted to first-past-the-post after winning the 1953 provincial election.[19]

2.3.2 Post-1950 Electoral Reform Concerns

From the 1950s to the mid-1970s, electoral reform debates were not as prominent as they were in the early 1900s. Nevertheless, some reforms took place. In 1960, the franchise was extended to First Nations peoples. Before this, First Nations peoples were permitted to vote only as long as they surrendered their "treaty rights and Indian status."[20] Following the 1960 amendment, First Nations peoples were permitted to vote without giving up their treaty rights. In 1968, Len Marchand became the first Aboriginal person elected to the House of Commons.[21]

In addition, academics would occasionally draw attention to the dysfunctional effects of the first-past-the-post system, as Alan Cairns did in an influential article published in 1968. According to Cairns, it has been "detrimental to national unity in Canada ... The electoral system has made a major contribution to the identification of particular sections/provinces with particular parties," because party elites make the conscious—and quite rational, under the existing rules of the political game—decision to direct the bulk of their organizational and financial resources to those regions in which they stand the best chance of winning.[22]

The relative silence of the electoral reform debate in the mid-1950s gave way to renewed reform interests in the late 1970s. In 1978, Prime Minister Pierre Trudeau created the Pepin–Robarts Task Force on Canadian Unity to make recommendations for dealing with the perceived threats to Canada's survival as a nation (Quebec separatism and western alienation being the chief ones). Although the Task Force on Canadian Unity viewed electoral reform as a comparatively minor issue—certainly less important than constitutional amending formulas, division of powers, and reform of the Senate—it nonetheless suggested that the size of the House of Commons be increased by about 60 members, and that additional seats to be awarded to candidates selected from party lists and distributed on the basis of a party's share of the national vote.[23] In its 1980 Speech from the Throne, the newly re-elected Liberal government of Pierre Trudeau promised to appoint a committee to study the electoral system; however, none was ever struck because opposition to even modest reforms among Members of Parliament was intense.[24]

More favourable conditions for electoral reform emerged in Quebec in the early 1980s.[25] The program of the Parti Québécois, which had first been elected in 1976, committed the government to implementing proportional representation. Premier René Lévesque viewed proportional representation as inherently more democratic than the first-past-the-post electoral system, which he considered to be conducive to petty patronage and corruption.[26]

Soon after its election in 1976, the Parti Québécois created a Ministry of State for Parliamentary and Electoral Reform, which was preoccupied during the government's first mandate with the reform of election financing—the Parti Québécois was the first administration in North America to outlaw corporate contributions to political parties—and with overseeing the referendum campaign. Robert Burns, the Minister responsible for electoral and parliamentary reform, issued a green paper in April 1979 in which he sketched out three possible alternatives for reforming the electoral system: list-PR in 28 multi-member regional ridings, a "mixed system" with two-thirds of the Members of the National Assembly elected by first-past-the-post in single-member ridings and the remainder elected in multi-member regional ridings, and a German-style system with a 50/50 split between first-past-the-post constituencies and list seats.[27]

At the beginning of the Parti Québécois' second mandate, its Ministry of State for Parliamentary and Electoral Reform proposed a list-PR system for Quebec. This proposal was endorsed, with slight modifications, by a commission under the direction of the province's chief electoral officer.[28] However, the Parti Québécois executive proposed a different model altogether. The disagreement between the party executive and the cabinet was never overcome, and the initiative for electoral reform dissipated in the run-up to the 1985 provincial election, which was won by the Quebec Liberal Party under Robert Bourassa.[29]

In 1982, the Trudeau government created a royal commission to investigate the challenges confronting the Canadian federation and its regions in the rapidly changing global economy. The Royal Commission on the Economic Union and Development Prospects for Canada, chaired by Donald S. Macdonald, former Minister of Finance in the Trudeau government, issued a three-volume report, accompanied by 72 volumes of research studies, in 1985. A number of the commission's recommendations dealt with the reform of Canada's political institutions, to strengthen government's capacity "to accommodate the internal social, economic and political diversity found within Canadian society. We seek to increase the responsiveness and effectiveness of public-policy making in a changing domestic and international environment."[30] The commissioners viewed electoral reform as "a second-best solution," after their preferred option, the creation of a Senate whose members would be elected by proportional representation. The report expressed scepticism about the use of proportional representation for elections to the House of Commons. Pure list-PR, in the view of the commissioners, would deprive Canadians of "the benefits of stable majority government," while a compensatory scheme modeled after the German electoral system would be prohibitively expensive and overly complicated. Such a system would also raise questions about two different classes of representatives sitting side-by-side in the House of Commons. The report concluded, "reform of the electoral system for the House of Commons is not practicable *at the present time*."[31]

More recently, the Royal Commission on Electoral Reform and Party Financing, established by the Mulroney government in 1989 and chaired by Pierre Lortie, specifically excluded any consideration of alternative electoral systems from its mandate. The final report suggested that the Royal Commission on the Economic Union and Development Prospects for Canada had "considered alternatives to our present system, including proportional representation, ... [b]ut so far none of these alternative systems has been placed before the House of Commons. We therefore do not recommend changes to this aspect of the electoral system, even though several interveners raised this issue at our public hearings."[32]

2.4 Current Reform Proposals

In this section we look at the issues and factors that characterize contemporary concerns with Canada's electoral system. In the past decade or so a number of political parties, both in power and in opposition, and at both the federal and provincial levels of government, have started to embrace the notion of reforming the existing first-past-the-post system. In addition to Quebec's Estates-General on the Reform of Democratic Institutions established in 2002, the Liberal government of Gordon Campbell in British Columbia recently established a Citizens' Assembly to hold public hearings and establish a citizens' committee to consider possible models for electing representatives to the provincial legislature, including preferential ballots and proportional representation. This Citizens' Assembly is non-partisan (current politicians and those who have recently served or run for public office are excluded from its membership) and in charge of its own governance and procedures. It will recommend one electoral model, and if the existing first-past-the-post system is not recommended, a referendum on the model proposed will be held in conjunction with the May 2005 provincial election.[33]

Prince Edward Island has also engaged in public consultations on the possibility of reforming its electoral system.[34] The debate over electoral reform included consideration of the relative merits of first-past-the-post versus proportional representation because the existing system has tended to produce overwhelming majorities for the winning party, thereby virtually excluding half—or more—of the electorate from meaningful or effective representation. In its discussion paper, the Prince Edward Island Commission on Electoral Reform notes that questions "are now being raised as to whether [first-past-the-post] is adequate for the 21st century or whether it should be changed so the composition of the Legislative Assembly would more accurately reflect the will of the electors."[35]

The Commission released its final report in December 2003. Although recognizing that many citizens expressed support for the existing voting system, the Commission submitted that a growing number of people believe it is time to examine the first-past-the-post voting system and whether it "meets the needs and desires of today's electorate." As the Commission noted, many citizens argue, "that under the present system every vote is counted but not every vote counts."[36] Overall, the Commission recommends that the first-past-the-post system be modified to include some element of proportionality, but also suggests that further consultation is necessary to "obtain a better reading as to what the general public really wants in the way of reform" to the first-past-the-post system.[37]

In Ontario, the recently elected Liberal Party has pledged to conduct a "full, open public debate" on voting reform, to be followed by a referendum on whether to keep the current system or replace it with another.[38] The Ontario New Democratic Party (2003) also supports a referendum on electoral system change.[39]

The recently elected Liberal government of Jean Charest in Quebec has pledged to introduce some element of proportionality into the electoral system within two years of its victory.[40] As part of its reform agenda to make democracy more representative and participatory, the Quebec government plans to develop new legislation that would reform the voting system.[41]

The Progressive Conservative Party in New Brunswick has established a "commission on legislative democracy to study the concept of proportional representation, fixed election dates and other mechanisms to ensure the full range of peoples' voices are represented in government and legislative debate and decision-making."[42] The commission was introduced in December 2003, and will produce its final report and recommendations in late 2004.

There has also been a marked increase in the past decade in the number of grassroots organizations advocating a new system of voting in Canada. Groups such as Democracy Watch (founded in 1993), the Mouvement pour une démocratie nouvelle (established in April 1999), and Fair Vote Canada (created in April 2001) have all raised concerns about the existing electoral system. The last organization has launched a public campaign, "Make Every Vote Count," aimed at educating voters about the defects of the present system and urging them to get involved in the electoral reform debate. The group has received support from both ends of the political spectrum, including such organizations as the Canadian Labour Congress and the Canadian Taxpayers Federation.[43] Women's groups such as Equal Voice also make arguments for reforming the electoral system as a way to improve women's representation.

Additionally, in September 2003, federal politicians weighed in on the electoral reform issue during a New Democratic Party-sponsored motion in the House of Commons, in which Members of Parliament were asked to vote on proportional representation. Although the New Democratic Party's motion to allow Canadians to vote on whether to change the current system to a more proportional system was defeated (144–76), the nature and scope of the debate signals a growing recognition of the need to seriously consider the merits of electoral reform. In addition to the New Democratic Party, the Conservative, Alliance, and Bloc Quebecois parties supported a process to review the current voting system.

It would thus appear that the last several years have witnessed considerable interest in electoral system reform in Canada. What accounts for this new momentum for change? There are new Canadian realities, such as a more mobile and diverse population, a declining voter turnout, decreasing youth participation, and recent electoral results that may help explain why change is viewed as necessary. There is also an international context that shapes our expectations toward politics and electoral reform.

2.4.1 Diversity and Representation

Canada inherited its electoral system from Great Britain in the late 19th century, at a time when society, and the meaning of representation, was vastly different than they are today. It was "designed at a time when the population was much more homogeneous and less mobile, so that where one lived very much defined one's political identity. The society that we live in today is much more mobile and has a multitude of identities and opinions that were not present, or were *disenfranchised*, when the [first-past-the-post] system was adopted in Canada."[44]

Despite the social gains that many groups may have made over the course of the 20th century, women, minority groups, and Aboriginal peoples still find themselves seriously under-represented among elected politicians. For example, although women constitute half of the Canadian population, they occupy one-fifth of the seats in the House of Commons. Internationally, Canada ranks 36th in terms of women's representation, placing well behind countries like Norway, Sweden, Finland, Denmark, Cuba, and Costa Rica, where women hold more than one-third of the seats in the lower house. In addition, minority groups constitute 11 percent, and Aboriginal peoples 3.5 percent of the population, although they constitute only 6 percent and 2 percent, respectively, of Members of Parliament.

Since the 1890s, when various women's suffrage associations fought for the extension of the franchise to women in Canada, many women's groups have favoured electoral reform as a strategy for improving women's representation in government. More recently, the Canadian Advisory Council on the Status of Women produced a study suggesting that the government consider a system of proportional representation because such a system would "pose fewer barriers to achieving representative outcomes than do single-member systems."[45] Equal Voice, a multipartisan action committee has created a website to sign up members interested in democratic reform, arguing that a country that elects only one woman for every five men is "out of touch with half its population and turning off equality-minded younger voters."[46] It has also produced a position paper calling for the replacement of Canada's "outmoded" electoral system with some form of proportional representation.[47]

The Royal Commission on Electoral Reform and Party Financing (Lortie Commission) recommended that the proportion of women in the House of Commons should be increased from 20 percent to 40 percent of legislators to provide for "equitable representation," within the context of the existing system.[48] The Royal Commission on Aboriginal Peoples recommended creating a separate Aboriginal parliament, or a "House of First Peoples," which would initially act as an advisory body,[49] but should eventually be provided with "the power to initiate legislation and to require a majority vote on matters critical to the lives of Aboriginal peoples."[50]

"Since Confederation, only 154 women have been elected to the House of Commons beginning with Agnes Macphail in 1921. In the last three federal elections, women's share of candidacies sharply declined from 476 in 1993 to 408 in 1997 to 373 in 2000. In Canada's 2000 federal election, women won only 39 out of the 172 seats that the governing Liberals attained. And out of 301 seats in the House of Commons as a whole, women occupied only 62 of them ... A modern democracy that still elects to our House of Commons only one woman for every five men is out of touch with half its population and turning off equality-minded younger voters. At the rate Canada is progressing, it will take ONE HUNDRED and SEVENTEEN years for women to achieve equity in the Canadian House of Commons."

M. McPhedran with R. Speirs, "Reducing the Democratic Deficit Through Equality-Based Electoral Reform," (Submission to the Law Commission of Canada, Spring 2003) at iv online: <http://www.equalvoice.ca/index.htm> (date accessed: 10 December 2003).

Along with the under-representation of different groups comes the absence of diverse voices and opinions in the system of democratic governance. Many observers suggest that the current first-past-the-post electoral system rewards large and established political parties, rendering it difficult for individuals or groups with new or different ideas, for example the environmental or peace movements, from participating in mainstream decision-making processes.[51] An example of the concern with a lack of "effective representation" is manifest in the Green Party of Canada's (and its former leader Joan Russow) recent constitutional challenge, in which the party argues that the current voting system discriminates against smaller parties, women, and racial and ethnic minorities.[52]

It is important to recognize that increased numbers of women, and greater representation of minority groups and Aboriginal people, in the House of Commons will not necessarily or automatically contribute to a greater diversity of voices or more "effective" representation in Parliament for their interests. As some observers remind us, greater representation of marginalized groups in the House of Commons would be a hollow achievement if they were not included in Cabinet decision-making processes.[53]

> "If Canadians want a Parliament with more women and Aboriginal MPs then the adoption of PR should be considered. But the experience of New Zealand and elsewhere suggests that selection of PR alone may be insufficient. Political Parties, even under PR, have to be committed to recruiting women and Aboriginal candidates, to placing these candidates high on the party-list and, once elected, to giving these MPs access to cabinet posts. It would also require the freeing up of party discipline on certain issues to make space for the representation of groups, rather than just partisan, interests."
>
> T. Arseneau, "The Representation of Women Under PR: Lessons from New Zealand" (November 1997) *Policy Options* at 12.

Perhaps one of the principal reasons that electoral reform is currently on the agenda in Canada is the increased pluralism of ideas that other systems of representation allow. In a very diverse and rapidly changing country, from a demographic and cultural perspective, the ability of the electoral system to represent the different voices is seen as very important for the legitimacy of the system. As the process of reviewing Quebec's democratic processes revealed, one of the main objectives of electoral reform should be to promote the entry of new voices into the political arena.[54] Voters who currently find the traditional parties to be merely slight variations on the same theme, and who thus lose interest in participating in the system, would likely be encouraged to get involved if new parties stood a realistic chance of gaining representation in the legislature.

For an increasing number of Canadians, the imbalances in our system of democracy are unacceptable. Indeed, the perceived barriers posed to the election of diverse groups by our first-past-the-post system, and the inability to accommodate a plurality of ideas, raise significant issues for our system of democratic governance. The desire to include a greater diversity of voices in the system of democratic governance is a growing concern for many citizens. Throughout our consultation process, the Commission heard from citizens who desire a system that better reflects the country's diverse population and ideas. Diverse representation represents one of the most important aspects of the electoral reform debate in Canada.

"… even though this [proportional representation] may not be … sufficient … to create favourable conditions for women, it may be a necessary condition …"

C. Maillé, Simone de Beauvoir Institute, Concordia University. Speaking at: Women's Representation in the House of Commons: *vox populis* (University of Ottawa, 31 October 2003).

2.4.2   Distorted Election Results

Another reason that electoral reform has assumed greater prominence in Canada over the past decade is found in the skewed results of the three most recent federal elections. As one electoral observer noted after the 1997 federal election, "the results of Canada's last two federal elections are becoming political science textbook cases of the distortions under [first-past-the-post],"[55] and the 2000 election did not deviate significantly from this trend. All three recent elections underscore just how fragmented the party system has become; in essence, it now consists of five distinct regional subsystems, with different dominant parties in each. The Liberals owe their dominant position partly to the workings of our electoral system, which, for example, translated 39 percent of the popular vote in the 1997 election into a majority (52 percent) of seats in the House of Commons. Moreover, in all three elections, the Liberal caucus was overwhelmingly dominated by its contingent from Ontario: since 1993, between 55 percent and 65 percent of the entire Liberal caucus has come from Ontario, where the party swept almost all of the seats in all three elections.[56]

This distortion has many observers claiming that the electoral system denies effective representation. For example, the aforementioned court challenge launched by the Green Party of Canada and its former leader, Joan Russow, contends that the *Canada Elections Act* is unconstitutional because, under Canada's first-past-the-post system, "the only voters who are represented by people who share their ideas about politics are those who cast ballots for candidates who received the most votes in a specific constituency. Voters who cast ballots for losing candidates are not represented by people with a commitment to the same principles and ideals. Their circumstances would be no different if they had wasted or spoiled their ballots."[57]

The Green Party also contends that the existing system violates the principle of the parity of voting power, which can be calculated by dividing the number of seats won by a party by the number of votes it received. On this measure, the Liberals in the 2000 election won a seat for every 30,184 votes their supporters cast. For the Bloc Québécois, this figure was 36,258, and for the Progressive Conservatives and the New Democratic Party, it was 130,582 and 84,134 respectively. "Rather than equality of voting power, Liberal votes were almost three times more valuable than those that were cast for the New Democratic Party and more than four times those that were marked for a Conservative."[58] The Green Party concludes that the election law violates sections 3 (right to vote and to effective representation) and 15 (equality rights) of the *Charter of Rights and Freedoms*.

In addition to the Green Party case, there have been several legal challenges relating to spending rules, party registration, or the definitions of electoral boundaries.[59] Cumulatively, these various court cases reflect a growing sentiment among many sections of the electorate that the existing electoral system is at odds with the prevailing democratic values, which place emphasis on effective representation of diverse groups and opinions.

2.4.3 Voter Turnout

Another reason that electoral reform has moved onto the political agenda in the past decade in Canada is that many scholars and politicians believe that a different method of voting might help to improve voter turnout. Turnout of registered voters in Canadian federal elections has been declining precipitously over the past decade. In the 2000 election, just over 61 percent of registered voters bothered to cast a ballot, the lowest figure for a federal election in Canadian history. If potential voters, or voting age population, were used to measure turnout, the figure would be even lower: 55 percent (see figure 4).[60] This places Canada in the bottom third of the thirty nations in the Organisation for Economic and Co-Operative Development (OECD) in terms of average voter turnout since 1945.[61]

Figure 4   Canadian voter turnout (as a percentage of the voting age population)

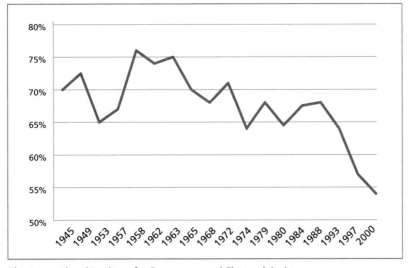

The International Institute for Democracy and Electoral Assistance, online: <www.idea.int/vt/region_view.efm?CountryCode=CA> (date accessed: 19 December 2003)

Advocates of proportional representation electoral systems contend that under the existing system, supporters of newer, non-traditional parties have little incentive to go to the polls, since their votes are, essentially, disregarded. "Some researchers have concluded that, other things being equal, countries that use a form of PR [proportional representation] tend to have higher turnout."[62] The positive impact of proportional representation electoral systems on turnout has been traced to the fostering of greater competition among party contenders:

"there can be no doubt that the dismal turnout (in the 1997 federal election in Canada) of only two-thirds of registered voters is linked to the fact that in most ridings only one or two of the parties were real contenders, with supporters of the others effectively disenfranchised."[63]

According to data compiled by the International Institute for Democracy and Electoral Assistance, electoral systems do have a modest impact on voter turnout: average turnout in plurality–majority systems (first-past-the-post), as well as in mixed or hybrid systems (proportional representation plus plurality, discussed in Chapter 4), is 59 percent to 60 percent, as opposed to 68 percent in straight proportional representation systems.[64] Recent Canadian research contends that turnout is "5 to 6 points higher in countries where the electoral system is proportional or mixed compensatory."[65] However, voter turnout has been dropping in the past decade in most OECD countries, including those with proportional representation systems, such as the Netherlands, Ireland, Finland, and Austria.[66] In short, a new Canadian electoral system with an element of proportional representation might boost voter turnout, but not significantly.

2.4.4 Youth Participation

Of particular concern in recent years has been the lack of youth participation in traditional political processes. For example, only about 25 percent of eligible voters between the ages of 18 and 24 cast ballots in the 2000 federal general election.[67] Although there is a range of factors contributing to the non-participation of youth, including a lack of knowledge about politics and insufficient time to vote, there is evidence to suggest that many youths do not feel connected to the system of democratic governance, or that they lack interest in politics.[68] Table 2, taken from a recent study completed in co-operation with Elections Canada, reveals some of the reasons that people provided when asked why young people did not vote in the 2000 election. As the table illustrates, one-third of people under the age of 25 cited disinterest and apathy as perceived reasons why youth did not vote, while two-fifths suggested that not feeling represented or connected played a role in the decision not to vote.

A youth forum co-sponsored by the Law Commission of Canada, Youth Canada Association (YouCAN!), the Toronto Youth Cabinet, and Elections Canada confirmed the importance of including a youth voice in political processes.[69] In addition to suggesting various ways of engaging youth in the traditional political process—including

Table 2   Perceived reasons why young people are less likely to vote

	Under 25 years old	25 and older
Not Integrated	**79**	**71**
Distanced from politics by age; not feeling represented, connected	40	37
Lack of information, understanding, knowledge	34	27
Lack of encouragement	2	4
Too busy, too mobile	3	3
Disengagement	**51**	**59**
Uninterested, apathetic	31	30
Negativism, cynicism, disillusionment	9	14
Distrustful of system, politicians	7	9
Irresponsibility, rebelliousness, laziness	4	6
Other	**2**	**4**
Do not know	**0**	*
N=	386	1,420

*less than 1 percent.

Reproduced from J. Pammett and L. LeDuc, "Confronting the Problem of Declining Voter Turnout Among Youth" (2003) 5:2 *Electoral Insight* at 6.

> "Young Canadians are not so much 'turned off' as 'tuned out'. They tend to be much less interested in politics than older Canadians and tend to know much less about what is going on politically. Interest in politics and political knowledge are two of the best predictors of who will vote and who will not."
>
> E. Gidengil, A. Blais, N. Nevitte and R. Nadeau, "Turned Off or Tuned Out? Youth Participation in Politics" (2003) 5:2 *Electoral Insight* at 11.

education programs, innovative voting methods (e.g., Internet voting), and lowering the voting age—many youths suggested that changing the electoral system to encourage a broader diversity of voices could be an important way of giving youth issues a greater presence in democratic governance. Of course, increasing the diversity of voices through a new electoral system does not guarantee piquing the interests of disengaged or marginalized groups, but the promotion of new political voices in and of itself constitutes one of the most important potential benefits of electoral reform.

2.4.5   International Precedents

International precedents have also moved electoral reform up the political agenda in the last decade or so. A process of international political learning is now taking place as institutional reforms in other jurisdictions catch the eye of politicians and the interested public in Canada. New Zealand, Italy, and Japan have all adopted new electoral systems in the past decade. Even the United Kingdom (birthplace of the single-member plurality electoral system now employed in Canada) has considered reform, setting up the Jenkins Commission in the late 1990s. The parliaments established in Scotland and Wales in 1999 both employ a mixed member proportional electoral system. As well, the newly established governments in several Soviet successor states have been engaged in a process of electoral system design over the past decade.[70] Interestingly, most of these countries have opted for some form of mixed electoral system such as mixed member proportional or an add-on system (such as mixed member majoritarian, discussed in Chapter 4). Some observers argue that the popularity of these systems and other mixed systems can be explained by the fact that they combine "the accountability strengths of plurality rule in single-member constituencies with the offsetting proportional qualities of regional or national lists."[71]

International reform efforts suggest that, in certain circumstances, the desire to improve democratic performance may outweigh the institutional and cultural inertia that militates against reform.

2.5 Electoral Reform and the Canadian Political Agenda

Canadians do have some historical experiences with electoral reform and related debates. The introduction of certain electoral reforms in western Canada in the 1930s, and the debates that took place in Quebec and at the federal level in the late 1970s and early 1980s, illustrate that some Canadians have struggled previously with questions about reforming the electoral system. The introduction of women's right to vote around the First World War and Aboriginal voting rights in the 1960s also provide examples of significant and important reforms to the Canadian electoral system.

In recent years, the electoral system has again come under close scrutiny for possible institutional innovation, particularly as an opportunity to invigorate Canadian democracy. This interest in electoral reform coincides with the recent experiences of a number of advanced industrial democracies, such as Japan, Italy, Scotland, Wales, and New Zealand, which have undertaken significant reforms of their electoral systems. Those advocating electoral reform in Canada contend that it is time to call into question the virtues of our first-past-the-post system, in particular its capacity to produce strong, single-party majority governments. Many suggest this alleged strength of our system has in fact led to a weakened opposition and an ineffective Parliament. Moreover, Canada's electoral system shows deficiencies in terms of representing diversity, both in terms of a diverse demographic and equitable representation of public opinion. In this regard, reformers argue it is time that our electoral system reflects the realities of the 21st century and more accurately represents the remarkable social and cultural diversity of our country.

Given the nature and extent of the electoral reform debates that are now occurring in many parts of the country, the question then becomes how to evaluate the current voting system and its alternatives. Chapter 3 provides an understanding of how we might go about evaluating the current system and deciding whether it is time for change.

---

1   A. Reynolds and B. Reilly, *The International IDEA Handbook of Electoral System Design*, 2nd ed. (Stockholm: International Institute for Democracy and Electoral Assistance, 1997) at 17.

2   According to Farrell, district magnitude (number of representatives elected in each riding) is the most important factor in determining proportionality: the larger the number of representatives elected in a given riding, the more proportional the overall results. The electoral formula itself is also important, but not as decisive. See, D.M. Farrell, *Comparing Electoral Systems* (London: Prentice Hall, 1997) at 144.

3   Reynolds and Reilly, *supra* note 1 at 61.

4   This is called the Droop Quota, and is calculated by the following formula: [total valid votes/(total number of seats) + 1] + 1. As an example: In a riding where 3 seats are to be won and 100 votes are cast, the quota would be [100/(3+1)]+1 or 26. So in order to be elected in this hypothetical riding, a candidate would have to win at least 26 percent of the vote. Example drawn from Farrell, *supra* note 2 at 117–19.

5   Reynolds and Reilly, *supra* note 1 at 83.

6   In some instances, a party may win a greater share of local candidate seats than its party vote percentage. We discuss this issue in greater detail in Chapter 4.

7   Parties typically place their "star" candidates at the top of the list, along with candidates from targeted groups (women, ethnic minorities, and Aboriginal people, for example) who might encounter difficulties being elected in a constituency campaign.

8   M.S. Shugart and M.P. Wattenberg, "Mixed-Member Systems: A Definition and Typology" in M.S. Shugart and M.P. Wattenberg, eds., *Mixed-Member*

Electoral Systems: The Best of Both Worlds? (Oxford: Oxford University Press, 2001) at 14.

9 A. Lijphart, "Trying to Have the Best of Both Worlds: Semi-Proportional and Mixed Systems" in A. Lijphart and B. Grofman, eds., *Choosing an Electoral System: Issues and Alternatives* (New York: Praeger, 1984) at 208–210.

10 S.R. Reed and M.S. Thies, "The Consequences of Electoral Reform in Japan" in M.S. Shugart and M.P. Wattenberg, eds., *Mixed-Member Electoral Systems: The Best of Both Worlds?* (Oxford: Oxford University Press, 2001) at 382.

11 Shugart and Wattenberg, *supra* note 8. For the numerous variations on these mixed or hybrid systems—there appear to be dozens of different types employed in the world today, if one includes systems operating in sub-national governments—see L. Massicotte and A. Blais "Mixed Electoral Systems: A Conceptual and Empirical Survey" (1998) 18:3 *Electoral Studies* at 341–66.

12 This section draws extensively on the work of D. Pilon, "The History of Voting System Reform In Canada" in H. Milner, ed., *Making Every Vote Count: Reassessing Canada's Electoral System* (Peterborough: Broadview Press, 1999) at 111–122; D. Pilon "Renewing Canadian Democracy: Citizen Engagement in Voting System Reform" (Ottawa: Law Commission of Canada, 2002); F.L. Seidle, *Electoral System Reform in Canada: Objectives, Advocacy and Implications for Governance* (Ottawa: Canadian Policy Research Networks Inc., 2002).

13 See J.C. Courtney, "Electoral Reform and Canada's Parties" in H. Milner, ed., *Making Every Vote Count: Reassessing Canada's Electoral System* (Peterborough: Broadview Press, 1999) at 91–100; see also Pilon, *ibid.*

14 Pilon, "The History of Voting System Reform in Canada", *supra* note 12 at 117.

15 *Canada: A History of the Vote in Canada* (Ottawa: Canadian Government Publishing–PWGSC, 1997) at 65.

16 *Ibid.* at 68.

17 Delayed in the sense that the adoption of proportional representation by governing conservative elites in order to prevent their own defeat at the hand of their socialist adversaries tended to occur much earlier—usually 20 to 30 years earlier—in most European nations than in Canada.

18 Pilon, "The History of Voting System Reform in Canada", *supra* note 12 at 116.

19 Pilon, "Renewing Canadian Democracy: Citizen Engagement in Voting System Reform", *supra* note 12 at 14.

20 Canada, *A History of the Vote in Canada, supra* note 15 at 85.

21 *Ibid.* at 88.

22 A. Cairns, "The Electoral System and the Party System in Canada, 1921–1965," in O. Kruhlak, R. Schultz and S. Pobihushchy, eds., *The Canadian Political Process,* rev. ed. (Toronto: Holt, Rinehart and Winston, 1973) at 133–58.

23 Canada, Task Force on Canadian Unity, *A Future Together: Observations and Recommendations* (Canada: Minister of Supply and Services, 1979) at 105–6.

24 Seidle, *supra* note 12 at 9.

25 H. Milner, "Obstacles to Electoral Reform in Canada" (1994) 24:1 *The American Review of Canadian Studies,* at 46.

26 It should be noted that this was Lévesque's personal view and does not necessarily reflect a sociological fact (namely, that first-past-the-post fosters more corruption than other electoral systems). In fact, political culture appears to play a much more determinant role in promoting patronage and corruption than does the electoral system.

27 Québec, Ministre d'État à la Réforme électorale et parlementaire (1979) at 113.

28 The main difference between the Ministry's proposal and that of the Chief Electoral Officer's commission was that the latter envisaged smaller multi-member districts. The province would be divided into 21 regional districts, with 3 to 14 seats per district.

29 Milner, *supra* note 25 at footnote 25.

30 Canada, Royal Commission on the Economic Union and Development Prospects for Canada, *Report: Volume Three* (Ottawa: Minister of Supply and Services, 1985) at 5.

31 *Ibid.* at 84–85. (Emphasis added.)

32 Canada, Royal Commission On Electoral Reform and Party Financing, *Final Report Volume I: Reforming Electoral Democracy* (Ottawa: Minister of Supply and Services, 1991) at 18.

33 G. Gibson, *Report on the Constitution of the Citizens' Assembly on Electoral Reform,* Vancouver (23 December 2002); N. Ruff, "BC Deliberative Democracy: The Citizens' Assembly and Electoral Reform 2003–2005" (Paper presented to the annual conference of the Canadian Political Science Association, 1 June 2003, Halifax).

34 This electoral reform initiative in Prince Edward Island followed a Charter challenge to the unique dual constituencies used in provincial elections. The basis of the complaint was that these constituencies violated section 3 of the Charter, which guarantees the right to vote—and, by implication, to "effective representation." *Re MacKinnon and Government of Prince Edward Island*, [1993] 101 D.L.R. (4th) 362 at 393–94 (P.E.I.S.C.[T.D.]), cited in J.A. Cousins, *Electoral Reform for Prince Edward Island: A Discussion Paper* (Charlottetown: Institute of Island Studies at the University of Prince Edward Island, 2000) at 20 and 35n.

35 Prince Edward Island, Electoral Reform Commission, *The Prince Edward Island Commission on Electoral Reform*, online: <http://www.gov.pe.ca/photos/original/elc_comm_reform.pdf > (date accessed: 19 December 2003) at i.

36 Prince Edward Island Electoral Reform Commission, [Final] *Report*, online: <http://www.gov.pe.ca/photos/original/er_premier2003.pdf> (date accessed: 30 January 2004) at 82.

37 *Ibid.* at 100–103.

38 Ontario Liberal Party, *Government that Works for You: The Ontario Liberal Plan for a More Democratic Ontario* (April 2003). As part of this process, the Premier, Dalton McGuinty, recently introduced the Minister Responsible for Democratic Renewal, Michael Bryant, who plans to engage Ontarians "in the most ambitious democratic renewal process in Ontario history" (Ontario, Ministry of the Attorney General and Democratic Renewal Secretariat, News Release, 8 December 2003).

39 As a number of critics have pointed out, however, it is the New Democratic Party in opposition that has embraced the idea of electoral reform; the New Democratic Party in power, in Manitoba and Saskatchewan, has not demonstrated much reforming zeal to date; nor did the recent New Democratic Party governments of Michael Harcourt and Glen Clark in British Columbia, or of Bob Rae in Ontario.

40 Quebec Liberal Party, "Making Voting System Reform a Priority." Brief presented to the Steering Committee for the General Consultation on the Reform of the Voting System of Quebec (November 2002) and Quebec Liberal Party, "A Necessary Reform of the Voting System." Brief presented to the Committee of Institutions of the National Assembly (November 2002).

41 Allocution de Monsieur Jacques P. Dupuis, Leader parlementaire du gouvernement Ministre délégué à la Réforme des institutions démocratiques et Ministre responsable de la région des Laurentides et de la région de Lanaudière.

IRPP Conference: The Reform of Democratic Institutions II, 10 September 2003, Montreal, Quebec. Also, see J.P. Dupuis (2003) « Réforme des institutions démocratiques : un projet en trois axes » 24:9 *Policy Options* at 6–8.

42 Progressive Conservative Party of New Brunswick, *Reaching Higher, Going Further* (2003) at 27.

43 Seidle, *supra* note 12 at 22–23.

44 T. Knight, "Unconstitutional Democracy? A Charter Challenge to Canada's Electoral System" (1999) 57:1 *University of Toronto Faculty Law Review* at 33. (Emphasis added.)

45 L. Young, "Electoral Systems and Representative Legislatures: Consideration of Alternative Electoral Systems" (Ottawa: Canadian Advisory Council on the Status of Women, 1994) at ii.

46 Equal Voice, "Equality-Based Electoral Reform" (2003), online: <http://www.equalvoice.ca/index.htm> (date accessed: 10 September 2003).

47 M. McPhedran with R. Speirs, "Reducing the Democratic Deficit Through Equality Based Electoral Reform" (Submission to the Law Commission of Canada, 2003) at iii, online: <http://www.equalvoice.ca/index.htm> (date accessed: 10 December 2003).

48 *Ibid.* at 221; Royal Commission on Electoral Reform and Party Financing, *supra* note 32 at 93–122.

49 Canada, *Report of the Royal Commission on Aboriginal Peoples: Restructuring the Relationship*, vol. 2 (Ottawa: Supply and Services Canada, 1996) at 379–380.

50 *Ibid.* at 377–78. The Royal Commission on Aboriginal Peoples was quite clear that the House of First Peoples should not be viewed as a substitute for Aboriginal self-government.

51 See, for example, H. MacIvor, "A Brief Introduction to Electoral Reform" in *Making Every Vote Count: Reassessing Canada's Electoral System* H. Milner ed. (Peterborough: Broadview Press, 1999) at 19–36.

52 See, *Russow v. Canada (A.G.)*, Court File No. 01-CV-210088 (Ont. S.C.J.), online: <http://www.law-lib.utoronto.ca/testcase/> (date accessed: 19 December 2003).

53 See, for example, T. Arseneau, "The Representation of Women and Aboriginals Under PR: Lessons From New Zealand" (November 1997) *Policy Options* at 12.

54 Québec, Comité directeur des États généraux sur la réforme des institutions démocratiques, *Prenez Votre Place! La participation citoyenne au Coeur des institutions démocratiques québécoises* (2003) at 25; cf. Seidle, *supra* note 12 at 28.

55 Milner, *supra* note 25 at 6.

56 Just over 58 percent of the Liberal caucus since the 2000 election comes from Ontario. For a discussion of these distortions, see B. Tanguay, "Canada's Political Parties in the 1990s: The Fraying of the Ties that Bind" in H. Lazar and T. McIntosh eds. *Canada: The State of the Federation 1998/99: How Canadians Connect* (Montreal and Kingston: McGill-Queen's University Press, 1999) at 217–44; B. Tanguay, "Political Parties and Canadian Democracy: Making Federalism Do the Heavy Lifting" in H. Bakvis and G. Skogstad eds. *Canadian Federalism: Performance, Effectiveness, and Legitimacy* (Toronto: Oxford University Press, 2002) at 296–316.

57 *Russow v. Canada (Attorney General)*, Court File No. 01-CV-210088 (Ont. S.C.J.) (Claimant's factum at para 7), online: <http://www.law-lib.utoronto.ca/testcase> (date accessed: 10 January 2004).

58 *Ibid.* at para 9.

59 Cousins, *supra* note 34 at 20.

60 The International Institute for Democracy and Electoral Assistance (IDEA), uses both registered voters and voting age population (all citizens above the legal voting age) to calculate turnout. According to the IDEA website, "the voting age population figures can provide a clearer picture of participation as they signal a problem with the voters' register or registration system … The register can under-represent the true size of the eligible voter pool if, as is often the case, it fails to record the names of new voters who have come of age or migrated to an area." See, the International Institute.for Democracy and Electoral Assistance, online: <www.idea.int> (date accessed: 19 December 2003). Blais, Massicotte and Dobrzynska note that both methods "have their biases," since calculations based on voting age population may "underestimate voter turnout, because the denominator is artificially swollen by people who are not entitled to vote." See, A. Blais, L. Massicotte and A. Dobrzynska "Why is Turnout Higher in Some Countries than in Others?" Paper presented to the Symposium on Electoral Participation in Canada. Ottawa: Carleton University, 18 February 2003 (Ottawa: Elections Canada) at 13. Online: <www.elections.ca/loi/tur/tuh/TurnoutHigher.pdf> (date accessed: 19 December 2003).

61 Ahead of, in order, France, Hungary, Luxembourg, Poland, Switzerland, the United States, and Mexico. Canada comes before the United States with its turnout of 49 percent in the 2000 presidential election. Canada's average voter turnout since 1945, based on voting age population, has been 68.4 percent, versus 48.3 percent in the United States and 48.1 percent in Mexico. Italy, with an average turnout of 92.5 percent, ranks number one among all 172 countries surveyed by the International Institute for Democracy and Electoral Assistance. Italy also has a system of compulsory voting, although IDEA notes that, somewhat surprisingly, "the 24 nations which have some element of compulsion associated with voting have only a small lead in turnout over the 147 nations without any compulsory laws." The difference in turnout between those countries with compulsory voting and those without would be higher if registered voters were used as the indicator. Blais et al argue that turnout is about 12 percentage points higher in countries with compulsory voting, *provided there is a penalty for not voting*. See, Blais, Massicotte and Dobrzynska *ibid.* at 1.

62 Seidle, *supra* note 12 at 28.

63 Milner, *supra* note 25 at 7.

64 Figures based on data compiled from 150 countries. See the International Institute for Democracy and Electoral Assistance, *supra* note 60.

65 Blais, Massicotte and Dobrzynska, *supra* note 60 at 1.

66 Seidle, *supra* note 12 at 28; M.P. Wattenberg, "The Decline of Party Mobilization" in R.J. Dalton and M.P. Wattenberg eds., *Parties Without Partisans: Political Change in Advanced Industrial Democracies* (New York: Oxford University Press, 2000) at 71.

67 J. Pammett and L. LeDuc, "Confronting the Problem of Declining Voter Turnout Among Youth" (2003) 5:2 *Electoral Insight* at 5.

68 See, for example, Pammett and LeDuc, *ibid.*; E. Gidengil, A. Blais, N. Nevitte and R. Nadeau, "Turned Off or Tuned Out? Youth Participation in Politics" (2003) 5:2 *Electoral Insight.*

69 The forum, "Ready, Set, Vote!" was held on 30 September 2003 in Toronto. It included more than 200 students from the Toronto region who shared their opinions and ideas regarding youth participation in the system of democratic governance, including issues relating to electoral reform and addressing low youth-voter turnout. The final report from the forum is available online: <www.youcan.ca> (date accessed: 30 January 2004).

70 Albania, Armenia, Azerbaijan, Croatia, Georgia, Lithuania, and Russia all adopted mixed or "parallel" electoral systems in the 1990s, combining proportional representation lists and winner-take-all ridings. However, unlike the German system, the proportional representation lists in these cases are not used to compensate for any disproportionate results in the constituency contests. See A. Reynolds and B. Reilly, *The International IDEA Handbook of Electoral System Design*, 2nd ed. (Stockholm: International Institute for Democracy and Electoral Assistance, 1997) at 55.

71 P. Dunleavy and H. Margetts, "Understanding the Dynamics of Electoral Reform" [1995] *International Political Science Review* 16 at 27, cited in D.M. Farrell, *Comparing Electoral Systems* (London: Prentice Hall, 1997) at 167.

Chapter 3 Democratic Values and the Choice of Electoral System

Chapter 3 evaluates the relevance and cogency of recent concerns with the electoral system by establishing a framework for evaluating Canada's first-past-the-post system and its alternatives. What criteria should we use to judge the current voting system? How should we choose between different electoral systems? How do we determine which system is "better"?

3.1 Systems and Values

Each of the main families of electoral systems reflects a different set of political values. In general, electoral formulas used in plurality–majority systems tend to produce legislative majorities. These systems (which include Canada's first-past-the-post system) typically encourage parties to be broad based and ideologically moderate. They are also supposed to produce two dominant parties that oscillate in and out of power, the party that loses the election forming a "government-in-waiting." The plurality–majority systems favour territorial ties between voters and their representatives.[1] By contrast, elections in proportional representation systems allow voters to have a diversity of opinions reflected in the legislature. They "are designed to produce the greatest proportionality in translating seats into votes, thus avoiding wasted votes and creating legislatures which closely mirror the political preferences of the electorate."[2] Hybrid, mixed or parallel systems seek to combine elements of plurality–majority and proportional representation systems.

Of course, there are additional values contained within proportional representation systems and plurality–majority systems. What is of particular concern for the current discussion is how to differentiate between the different values, and how they relate to the Canadian context. To help us with this, we now turn to the criteria that have been used by electoral system engineers to explore different models for translating votes into seats, as well as to the comments and feedback the Commission received from citizens during its engagement process.

3.2 Evaluating Electoral Systems

Electoral systems can be evaluated both on empirical and normative grounds. Empirical judgments can be made about the likely consequences (in terms of costs, effectiveness, representativeness) of the various possible types of electoral systems, while normative judgments concern how "'good' or 'bad,' and 'important' or 'trivial' these consequences are."[3] There is certainly no foolproof algorithm for determining the superiority of a given electoral system over its alternatives. As well, no electoral system can simultaneously promote all the different democratic values cherished by a society. There will necessarily be trade-offs or tensions between key values. At different times, particular political cultures will embrace some values over others, and these values are likely to change over time.

Recent Canadian research by Bryan Schwartz and Darla Rettie used the work of the New Zealand Royal Commission, along with the International Institute for Democracy and Electoral Assistance's *Handbook of Electoral System Design*, to compile a list of 13 criteria for evaluating competing electoral models.[4] An electoral system, in their view, ought to promote 13 qualities.

- **The geographical or territorial representation of voters:** Each area, such as a riding, should elect representatives who are accountable to that area.

- **Fairness:** The representation of political parties should adequately reflect the diversity of opinion in society—"if half the voters vote for one political party but that party wins no, or hardly any, seats in parliament, then that system cannot be said to adequately represent the will of the people."[5]

- **Demographic representation:** The legislature should, to the extent that it is practicable, be a "mirror of the nation,"

New Zealand's Royal Commission on the Electoral System developed a set of ten criteria to evaluate the first-past-the-post system and its alternatives. These criteria were:

- fairness between political parties, which can be measured by the proportionality between a party's seats and votes;

- effective representation of minority and special interest groups;

- effective Maori representation;

- political integration, that is, the facilitation of consensus-building and the promotion of respect for diverse opinions;

- effective representation of constituents;

- effective voter participation;

- effective government;

- effective Parliament;

- effective parties; and

- legitimacy—citizens should view the system as being legitimate.

Using these ten criteria, the Royal Commission concluded that the mixed member proportional and single transferable vote systems were both superior to first-past-the-post on all of the different indicators, with the exception of the effective representation of constituents—the territorial ties between voters and their elected representatives being one of the chief virtues of first-past-the-post—and effective government, on which all three systems were more or less equal. In the end, the Royal Commission felt that a German-style mixed member proportional system would be most suitable for New Zealand.

New Zealand, Royal Commission on the Electoral System,
Towards a Better Democracy (Wellington: Government Printer, 1986).

including both men and women and the various religious, ethnic and linguistic communities that comprise a society.

- **Accessibility:** It should be easy to cast a vote, meaning that it is not unduly difficult to register, and the ballot should not be confusing. Furthermore, the ballot should be secret, so that choices may be expressed freely and without the threat of coercion or reprisal.

- **Meaningfulness:** The voters should know that their ballot makes a difference to the final result. Systems in which there are many *wasted votes*—votes that do not have any impact on the final result because it is a "winner-take-all" system—mean that the second and third place candidates or parties receive no legislative pay-off even when they obtain a large share of the vote.

- **One person–one vote:** Each vote should have roughly the same weight.

- **An effective legislature:** An effective legislature has real power to pass laws and scrutinize the government's actions.

- **Accountability:** Voters should be able to hold elected members accountable for their actions in the legislature or in government.

- **Consensus-building:** An electoral system should help lessen tensions in society by rewarding candidates who can appeal to more than a narrow constituency.

- **Stable and effective government:** This means a government that is able to enact its electoral program.

- **An effective parliamentary opposition:** An opposition should be able to critically assess legislation and present an alternative to the incumbent government. The electoral system should prevent the development of a winner-take-all attitude, one which leaves the governing party blind to other views and the needs of opposition voters.

- **Ease of administration:** The electoral system should not be overly expensive or difficult to administer.

- **Ease of transition:** The government must be easily able to oversee the transition from an existing system to any new electoral model. The more foreign the system, the more difficult reform will be.

The authors also conducted a review of the academic literature on electoral reform in Canada (written since 1979) to determine which of these 13 values seemed to be most important, in terms of frequency, to the various authors.[6] Demographic representation (the legislature as mirror of the nation) and fairness (proportionality between a party's share of the vote and its representation in the legislature) were the top-ranked criteria, based on these expert views. Development of truly national parties, stable and effective government, geographical representation, minimizing wasted votes and government accountability were also important.

> "[first-past-the-post] ... is severely defective when judged by at least three criteria that Canadians have identified as key electoral criteria. One is that, in principle, there should be a reasonable correspondence between voter support for a party and the number of seats it actually wins. The current system often produces drastic inequities in this regard. Another is that a system should encourage parties to find creative solutions that bring people together. The current system tends instead to be destructive of national unity. It encourages some parties to focus their efforts on a few regions of core support, and to play upon regional grievances. A third is that the system should produce a parliament that is geographically representative. The current system often leaves some provinces or regions without any elected members in the governing party."
>
> B. Schwartz and D. Rettie, "Valuing Canadians: The Options for Voting System Reform in Canada" (Ottawa: Law Commission of Canada, 2002) at 70.

3.3 Criteria for Evaluating Electoral Systems

Many citizens who participated in the Commission's electoral reform consultation process echoed many of the values and criteria outlined above. In addition to raising general questions and arguments about disregarded votes and the "legitimacy" of Canada's first-past-the-post electoral system, the Commission heard from a number of Canadians who expressed concern with a lack of effective representation. Of particular interest was a lack of diverse representation, both in terms of demographics—representation of women, minority groups, and Aboriginal people—and ideas, or the notion that Parliament would greatly benefit from the inclusion of a plurality of voices. In addition, many citizens expressed distaste with the adversarial political decision making, especially negative campaigning both before and after elections. Instead, they hoped for a democracy based upon more cooperation and consensus building to effectively address important policy issues and concerns.

Building on the existing literature, as well as the feedback and input received through its consultation process, the Commission has established a list of ten criteria to evaluate Canada's first-past-the-post voting system. (Table 3 lists these criteria.)

Table 3   Ten criteria for assessing electoral systems

• representation of parties
• demographic representation
• diversity of ideas
• geographic representation
• effective government
• accountable government
• effective opposition
• valuing votes
• regional balance
• inclusive decision making

3.3.1 Representation of Parties

An electoral system is fair, or representative of political parties and the political situation in the country, if each party's contingent in the legislature is roughly proportionate to its voting strength. Since 1945, election results in federal elections in Canada have been among the most *disproportionate* in the established democracies. Farrell ranks Canada 35th out of 37 democracies in terms of proportionality (the correspondence between a party's share of the seats in the legislature and its share of the vote).[7]

It is well established that parties with regionally concentrated support are rewarded with representation in Parliament that far exceeds their share of the national popular vote, while parties with support distributed across the country typically receive fewer seats than they deserve.[8] For example, it is possible for a party to win a majority of the seats in a legislature while placing second in terms of percentage of votes received.

There are several examples at both the federal and provincial levels of election results that distort the translation of votes into seats. In 1997, for example, the Liberal Party captured a majority of the seats with less than a majority of the vote. Similarly, in 1990, the Ontario New Democratic Party captured 57.7 percent of the seats with 37.6 percent of the popular vote. In 2000, the Progressive Conservative Party of Prince Edward Island captured 96.3 percent of the seats with 57.9 percent of the popular vote.[9]

The limited survey data available indicates that a majority of Canadian voters have difficulties with the first-past-the-post voting system. Howe and Northrup's research indicates that a majority of voters believe that the first-past-the-post electoral system is "unfair" or "unacceptable," in particular the fact that a party can win a majority of the seats and form a majority government without winning a majority of the vote (See Chapter 1, figure 1).[10] Although other research suggests that a majority of Canadians have difficulties understanding the current system,[11] it does not detract from the point that an increasing number of citizens have problems with the results produced through the existing system.

3.3.2 Demographic Representation

Demographic representation refers to the importance of an electoral system that broadly represents the diversity of people in society, including women, minority groups, and Aboriginal people. As the Commission heard throughout its consultation process, Parliament and provincial legislatures should, as much as possible, reflect the composition of society. Schwartz and Rettie's analysis echoes this sentiment, noting, "the parliament should, to some degree, be a 'mirror of the nation'. It should include both men and women and reflect various religious affiliations, linguistic communities and ethnic groups."[12]

On the criterion of demographic representation, first-past-the-post performs poorly. If we measure the representation of women in terms of the percentage elected to the lower house in various countries, Canada, with 21 percent female legislators, ranks 36th in the world, after most of the European countries and Australia, but ahead of France, the United States, and the United Kingdom.[13] Plurality and majoritarian electoral systems, on the whole, seem to present more obstacles to the election of women candidates than either list-PR or mixed member proportional systems.[14] As the data in table 4 show, the proportion of women elected to the legislature in countries using list-PR electoral systems is about 9 percentage points higher than in countries using a mixed member proportional system (28.9 percent versus 19.8 percent), which in turn is about 2 percentage points higher than in countries with first-past-the-post systems. Statistically, the difference between first-past-the-post and mixed member proportional systems on this indicator is not huge. However, Arseneau, examining the experience of New Zealand after it adopted a mixed member proportional system in the mid-1990s, shows that the first election conducted under this system, in 1996, resulted in a "record number of women and Maori Members of Parliament."[15] Most important, from her perspective, was that women and Maori candidates tended to be most successful in the list (compensatory) seats.

Approximately a third of Canadian voters in 2000 believed that the under-representation of women in the House of Commons constituted a problem.[16] Electoral reform that brings some element of

Table 4 Percent of women legislators in lower houses of advanced industrial democracies, 2003

Electoral System	Country legislators	% women	Average (mean)
List-PR	Sweden	45.3	
	Denmark	38.0	
	Finland	37.5	
	Netherlands	36.7	
	Norway	36.4	
	Belgium	35.3	
	Austria	33.9	28.9
	Iceland	30.2	
	Spain	28.3	
	Switzerland	23.0	
	Portugal	19.1	
	Luxembourg	16.7	
	Israel	15.0	
	Greece	8.7	
STV	Ireland	13.3	10.5
	Malta	7.7	
MMP	Germany	32.2	
	New Zealand	28.3	19.8
	Italy	11.5	
	Japan (MMM)	7.3	
FPTP	*CANADA*	*20.6*	
	United Kingdom	17.9	17.6
	United States	14.3	
Majoritarian	Australia	25.3	18.8
	France	12.2	
All PR/Semi-PR FPTP/Majoritarian	(N=20)		19.7
	(N=5)		18.2

Adapted from D. Studlar, "Will Canada Seriously Consider Electoral Reform? Women and Aboriginals Should" in H. Milner ed., *Making Every Vote Count: Reassessing Canada's Electoral System* (Peterborough: Broadview Press, 1999) at 129, table 10-1. Data for 2003 compiled from the Inter-Parliamentary Union website <http://ipu.org/wmn-e/classif.htm> (date accessed: 19 December 2003).

proportionality into our existing system would undoubtedly ameliorate the situation, though to what extent remains to be seen. Some observers point out that while the proportion of female legislators in New Zealand increased after the adoption of a mixed member proportional system, the percentage of women in cabinet positions actually dropped.[17] Therefore, proportional representation alone may not be sufficient for securing effective representation. Nevertheless, adding an element of proportionality to the electoral system could improve the representation of women in the House of Commons.

Women are not the only group to be disadvantaged by first-past-the-post and under-represented in Canada's legislatures. Ethnic minorities and Aboriginal peoples also have fewer representatives than their share of the population warrants: they constituted 11 percent and 3.5 percent, respectively, of the Canadian population in 1996, but only 6 percent and 2 percent of Members of Parliament.[18] As with the under-representation of women, some 35 percent of Canadian voters find the under-representation of minority groups to be cause for concern, and nearly half of voters are favourable to measures that would increase the number of minority candidates running for office.[19] With respect to Aboriginal peoples, 57 percent of respondents favoured creating seats in Parliament for Aboriginal representatives.[20] (Figure 5 illustrates these results.)

The advantage that proportional representation systems have over first-past-the-post in promoting demographic representation stems from the fact that the lists drawn up for compensatory seats (in mixed member proportional) or multi-member districts (list-PR) can be used to place women and minority candidates in a less difficult position, making their election more likely (it could allow for a form of affirmative action).[21] At the very least, proportional representation systems "pose fewer barriers to achieving demographically representative outcomes than do single member systems."[22]

Figure 5 Opinions of Canadians on measures to improve representation of various groups in Parliament

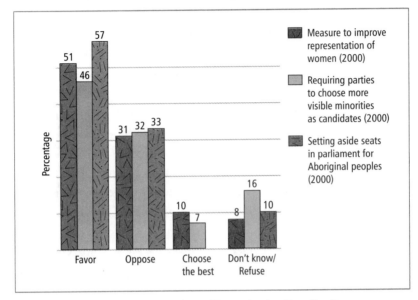

Adopted from P. Howe and D. Northrup, "Strengthening Canadian Democracy: The Views of Canadians" (2000) 1:5 *Policy Matters* at 18–20. The category "choose the best" refers to "choose the best candidate." It does not apply to seats for Aboriginal peoples.

> "There are many factors that account for public alienation from the system of government. A key factor is the tendency for elections to produce 'manufactured' majorities that in fact lack the support of most voters and then proceed to implement policies that do not reflect widely held values and preferences."
>
> Stephen Phillips, Vancouver. Feedback from the Law Commission of Canada's consultation process. (Received: 14 April 2003.)

3.3.3 Diversity of Ideas

Integrally linked to the criteria of demographic and geographic representation is the notion of supporting a plurality of ideas. For legislatures to represent broadly the wishes of the electorate, electoral systems should attempt to reflect the diversity of ideas and interests of its citizens. As outlined in Chapter 2, a prominent reason that electoral reform is currently on the agenda in Canada is that citizens desire the inclusion of a broader diversity of voices in the system of democratic governance. The ability of the electoral system to represent the different voices in a country is seen as important for the legitimacy of the system.

Canada's first-past-the-post electoral system fails to incorporate a broad enough diversity of ideas into the decision-making process. The argument in this case is that small or nationally-based parties (such as the Green Party of Canada) have difficulty winning seats in Parliament, therefore only an overly narrow selection of ideas from the dominant party make it into the policy and legislative decision-making process. At the same time, there is also a growing concern that the system does not account for the interests and ideas of a broad range of Canadians, as evidenced by the lack of youth voice and interest in mainstream political processes. If "accommodating difference is what Canada is all about"[23]—something the Commission heard throughout our consultations—then the present electoral system does not appear to be up to the job of ensuring that the diversity of society and its ideas are adequately reflected in the system of democratic governance. In fact, Canada's first-past-the-post system appears to perform poorly when it comes to this increasingly important criterion.

"It is urgent that the voting system in Canada be reformed so that ALL citizens are represented in parliament. The current system effectively disenfranchises those whose views are not represented by the majority party in any particular riding. A fair voting system is the only way that all the citizens of Canada will have fair representation. The 'first-past-the-post' electoral system is archaic, and has been abandoned in most countries of the world, and it is time for Canada to do the same."

Paul van Oosten, Calgary. Feedback from the Law Commission of Canada's consultation process. (Received: 11 May 2003.)

3.3.4   Geographic Representation

Geographic representation refers to the ability of voters to elect a representative to Parliament or a provincial legislature who is "ultimately accountable to that area."[24] Geographic representation is typically viewed as a chief strength of Canada's plurality system. First-past-the-post promotes geographic representation, a strong and clear link between voters in a particular constituency and their representative. For many observers, the ability of voters to know who to contact when they have a "personal or local concern" is one of first-past-the-post's strongest features.[25]

While geographic representation is one of first-past-the-post's strengths, it is also an issue of growing concern. First, the limited research on geographic representation suggests that the link between constituents and their elected representatives may not be as important as we initially thought. For example, research from the United Kingdom suggests that the "closeness of the MP–constituency link is usually exaggerated…"[26] evidenced by the fact that approximately 50 percent of the population could not name their Member of Parliament, and only 10 percent had contacted their Member of Parliament in the past five years.[27] Although this should not undermine the important link between constituents and Members of Parliament, it does suggest that this often cited virtue of the first-past-the-post system is not without need for improvement or reform.

Second, at various points throughout the Commission's consultation process, we heard from citizens who suggested that although the link between constituents and Members of Parliament is important, this concept might not fully reflect contemporary Canadian values and experiences. Today's highly mobile and diverse citizens often identify themselves with communities of interest that are not geographically determined, or that lie outside their community of residence. It may therefore be somewhat limiting to conceptualize our electoral system primarily on the basis of territorial constituencies. Perhaps it is time to consider reforms that balance both the value of direct representation and the desire to incorporate extra-geographical interests into the system of democratic governance.

3.3.5   Effective Government

Effectiveness refers to the ability of governments to develop and implement various legislative and policy agendas.[28] As Blais notes in his analysis of criteria for assessing electoral systems, "[w]e want an *effective* government, a government that is capable of effectively managing the state."[29] First-past-the-post tends to produce effective majority governments that can "exercise energetic and innovative leadership throughout their mandate and can proceed with a coherent agenda. They can take bold, and at times unpopular individual measures…"[30] This is certainly true of Canada: in the 37 general elections held since 1867, a single party has won a majority of the seats 29 times.[31] Of course, it is possible that first-past-the-post provides too much of a good thing in Canada in that majority governments can produce weak oppositions. Far from being the virtue that it was held to be in the 1950s, the first-past-the-post tendency to yield majority governments is now being criticized as an important factor contributing to the democratic deficit, since it diminishes the effectiveness of Parliament and provincial legislatures.[32] Nevertheless, effective government is an important value for Canadians in a context of an increasingly complex international situation.

3.3.6   Accountable Government

The accountability criterion refers to the ability of voters to identify policy makers, to hold them accountable for their decisions while in office and, if need be, to remove them from office. "Once elected, legislators are free to do what they want. But electors are able not to re-elect them if they feel their representatives have not done a good job. This creates an incentive for representatives to be sensitive to the views of their constituents."[33] This has long been a positive feature of Canada's plurality electoral system (first-past-the-post), but it must be noted that in the past decade, with the fragmentation of the national party system and the disappearance of a united opposition that could be seen by voters as a viable "government-in-waiting", growing numbers of voters have found it difficult to "vote out" parties or Members of Parliament when they are unhappy with an incumbent government's performance, since they see no alternative to replace the party in power.

3.3.7 Effective Opposition

Closely linked to effectiveness and accountability is the desire for a system to encourage an "effective" opposition. "The electoral system should help to ensure the presence of [...an...] opposition that can critically assess legislation and present an alternative to the current government."[34] Since Canada's first-past-the-post electoral system promotes majority governments, opposition parties are often at a loss to challenge policy and legislation that they may deem to be ineffective or counterproductive. "A party can often win an outright majority by establishing and maintaining a core vote of about 40%, almost reducing to zero the need to accommodate any other party."[35]

In addition, with the occasionally massive voter swings that occur as a result of the first-past-the-post system, some parties are unnecessarily reduced to an almost non-existent presence in the political process. Recent examples of this can be found at both the provincial and federal levels. For example, following the 2001 provincial general election in British Columbia, the New Democratic Party received 21.5 percent of the popular vote, but only won 2 of 79 seats in the legislature. The Liberal Party won the remaining 77 seats. At the federal level, the Progressive Conservative Party went from 169 seats in the House of Commons to just 2 seats following the 1993 general election, despite the fact that they received 16 percent of the popular vote. This is not to suggest that these parties should have remained in office (in both cases there was considerable appetite among voters to change the status quo) but that the extent of their defeat was exaggerated and, in the process, contributed to "ineffective" opposition in Parliament.

3.3.8 Valuing Votes

If voters believe that their votes do not factor into the election results, then they are less likely to participate in elections.[36] For example, it has been argued that voters who cast their ballots in an election for a losing candidate are considered to have their votes disregarded. And while it is difficult to totally address the issue of disregarded votes— for example, even in proportional systems, a candidate or party may be excluded from decision-making processes—it is important to minimize this problem to the greatest extent possible. Voting is one of the ways in which citizens express themselves politically, and it is indicative of the voice that voters would like to have reflected in the system of democratic governance.

> "Under our current voting system, our votes only count—or have impact on the allocation of seats—when we happen to share the most popular partisan viewpoint in our riding. In other words, what you believe in determines whether your vote counts—not the fact that you're an equal citizen along with everyone else in your riding."
>
> *Make Every Vote Count* (2003), available from Fair Vote Canada. For contact information visit: <http://www.fairvotecanada.org>.

The first-past-the-post system does not do a good job of minimizing disregarded votes. Indeed, many observers claim that in our electoral system most votes are disregarded.[37] Table 5 illustrates a typical first-past-the-post election result. In this scenario, the White Party wins a majority of seats in the legislature or House of Commons, despite the fact that more than 60 percent of the voters selected a different candidate. Many observers, including those who participated in the Commission's consultation process, suggest that people who do not vote for the winning party have little input into the political decision-making process, and are in the process becoming disconnected from politics.[38]

In addition, the phenomenon of disregarded votes has contributed to strategic voting, in which voters cast their ballots for candidates of parties that they do not prefer, simply to prevent a more disliked alternative from winning a seat. Some researchers estimate that strategic voting can be as high as 30 percent in some elections.[39]

Table 5   Example of a common first-past-the-post election result

Party Name	Percentage of Popular Vote	Percentage of Seats Won
Red	11	15
White	39	52
Blue	11	7
Green	19	7
Orange	20	19
Total	100	100

3.3.9   Regional Balance

In a country as geographically diverse as Canada, it is important to have all parts of the country represented in the system of democratic governance and its related decision-making processes. The system should not disadvantage parties with well-distributed national support while encouraging those with regionally-concentrated support.[40] A familiar concern with Canada's first-past-the-post electoral system is that it encourages regionally-based politics. Writing in the late 1960s, Professor Alan Cairns asserted that the electoral system in Canada exacerbates regional and ethno-linguistic cleavages by offering parties incentives to promote tensions related to religion, nationalism, and regionalism.[41] According to Cairns' argument, first-past-the-post benefits regionally-concentrated parties in a way that does not accurately reflect their total share of the national popular vote. Parties that enjoy strong support in a given region are more likely to translate this support into a seat win. Meanwhile, parties without a regional base who try to mount a national strategy are systematically disadvantaged by the electoral system, as their support is often too diffuse to translate into a plurality in a given riding. While a party can enjoy respectable standing in the overall national, popular vote, if this support amounts to a second-best standing in every riding, this party is shut out of Parliament altogether.

A further consequence identified by Cairns is the electoral strategies that the first-past-the-post system promotes. Given that relatively lower support in some regions of the country will not translate into seat gains in the House of Commons, some parties choose to ignore these regions and concentrate on those that rendered more fruitful results.[42] The 1957 election strategy of the Progressive Conservatives is illustrative. Determining that it was unlikely that they would win seats in Quebec with the number of votes they stood to gain, the Conservatives chose to focus their campaign efforts on more winnable regions, which reinforced the notion that they were not a "Quebec" party. The primary effect of the electoral system, then, is that parties may tailor their election campaigns, policies, and platforms to appeal to sectional blocs where their support is strong or where they need support.[43] Elections,

---

"One of the great disadvantages of the FPTP system is, in my opinion, that it encourages confrontation rather than consultation and compromise. As well, a new Government can undo what a previous Government achieved, and start from scratch, rather than retain the good elements of previous legislation and in consultation tries as much as possible to preserve a continuum. The flip-flop of one dominant party to another is against democratic principles in that it ignores the variety of voices, which especially in Canada with its multi-cultural society, deserves to be heard, to be taken into account and, in fact, taken advantage of. What a wonderful input of ideas and experiences is lost under the current system!"

Ruth Mechanicus, Toronto. Feedback from the Law Commission of Canada's consultation process. (Received: 21 February 2003.)

"There is indeed a very serious democratic malaise or deficiency in Canada, as reflected in declining voter participation in elections, inadequate representation of women and minorities, and election results that bear little resemblance to the pattern of voting. Perhaps the biggest single cause of these problems is our antiquated voting system."

Bryce Kendrick, Sidney, British Columbia. Feedback from Law Commission of Canada's consultation process. (Received: 24 November 2002.)

Cairns argued, are essentially contests between regions rather than contests between parties.[44]

Another effect of this reinforcing cycle is the lack of representation afforded to certain regions of the country in Cabinet. Those regions that are not represented in Cabinet may be denied the opportunity to voice effectively regional concerns. The perspective of the governing party becomes slanted to those regions where their share of the vote has translated into seats and/or a Cabinet position.[45] The cumulative effect of this, notes Cairns, will shape the values and culture of this political party. Further, the ability of the governing party to be truly representative of national interests is compromised.

It is important to acknowledge that parties have always had difficulty in achieving balanced regional representation within the House of Commons—and that this is inevitable in a country as geographically and ideologically diverse as Canada. We should not overestimate the independent contribution of the electoral system to the emergence of regional misunderstanding and conflict. At the same time, however, it should not detract from the position that the electoral system plays some role in preventing nationally-based political parties from being represented in Parliament.

3.3.10 Inclusive Decision Making

Linked to concerns about regionalism is the desire for a more consensual style of decision making in politics. Many Canadians would like to see a more inclusive style of politics, one that incorporates a diversity of opinions and ideas. Part of Cairns' thesis is that the first-past-the-post system promotes regionalism, which in turn contributes to regionally-based adversarial politics in the House of Commons.[46] In addition, recent and increasing demands for a broader diversity of people and voices in Parliament reflect the desire for more inclusive decision-making processes in government. In many ways, "… we hope that governments will try hard to find compromises in order to avoid social conflicts from becoming too divisive. We want governments to manifest a *sense of accommodation*."[47] Echoing this sentiment, many citizens who participated in the Commission's consultation process espoused the goal of a more inclusive style of decision making.

3.4 First-past-the-post: Time for Change

The first-past-the-post system performs poorly on many criteria for evaluating electoral systems, including criteria that are considered traditional strengths of the first-past-the-post system. This negative scorecard conforms in large part to the majority sentiments of individuals whom we heard from during our consultation process— that it is time to seriously consider reforming Canada's electoral system. In this case, the question now becomes what different voting systems are suitable for the Canadian context?

Before advocating what we believe would be a better electoral system for Canada, that is, one most likely to achieve most (but not all, since no electoral system is perfect) of the democratic values cherished by Canadians, we must examine the alternatives and improvements to the first-past-the-post electoral system and provide an assessment of their relative strengths and weaknesses.

Table 6 Assessment of the first-past-the-post voting system

Criteria	FPTP
1. Representation of Parties	
2. Demographic Representation	
3. Geographic Representation	✔
4. Diversity of Ideas	
5. Effective Government	✔
6. Accountable Government	✔
7. Effective Opposition	
8. Valuing Votes	
9. Regional Balance	
10. Inclusive Decision Making	

Note: A ✔ represents strengths or potential strength. The absence of a ✔ does not suggest a total lack of this criterion, but rather our analysis indicates that it is not immediately evident if this criterion could be met in the Canadian context.

1   D. Butler, "Electoral Systems" in D. Butler, H.R. Penniman and A. Ranney eds., *Democracy at the Polls: A Comparative Study of Competitive National Elections* (Washington: American Enterprise Institute, 1981) at 18–21.

2   H. MacIvor, "A Brief Introduction to Electoral Reform" in H. Milner ed., *Making Every Vote Count: Reassessing Canada's Electoral System* (Peterborough: Broadview Press, 1999) at 26.

3   A. Blais, "Criteria for Assessing Electoral Systems" (1999) 1:1 *Electoral Insight* at 3.

4   *Ibid.* at 11–14; B. Schwartz and D. Rettie, *Valuing Canadians: The Options for Voting System Reform in Canada* (Ottawa: Law Commission of Canada, 2002); A. Reynolds and B. Reilly, *The International IDEA Handbook of Electoral System Design*, 2nd ed. (Stockholm: International Institute for Democracy and Electoral Assistance, 1997) at 9–14.

5   Reynolds and Reilly, *ibid.* at 9.

6   Schwartz and Rettie, *supra* note 4 at 39–41.

7   D.M. Farrell, *Comparing Electoral Systems* (London: Prentice Hall, 1997). See also L. LeDuc, "New Challenges Require New Thinking about Our Antiquated Electoral System" in H. Milner ed., *Making Every Vote Count: Reassessing Canada's Electoral System* (Peterborough: Broadview Press, 1999) at 65–70. LeDuc, using the same Index of Disproportionality as Farrell, ranks the 1993 federal election in Canada as the second most disproportionate result since 1968 among 11 countries (France, the United Kingdom, the United States, Australia, New Zealand, Germany, Italy, Japan, Sweden, and Belgium were the other countries in the comparison). The 1997 election was the 4th most disproportionate.

8   A. Cairns, "The Electoral System and the Party System in Canada, 1921–1965" in O. Kruhlak, R. Schultz and S. Pobihushchy eds., *The Canadian Political Process*, rev. ed. (Toronto: Holt, Rinehart and Winston, 1973) at 133.

9   Fair Vote Canada, *Dubious Democracy Report* (September 2003) online: <http://www.fairvotecanada.org/updir/Dubious_Democracy_Report.pdf> (date accessed: 15 December 2003).

10 P. Howe and D. Northrup, "Strengthening Canadian Democracy: The Views of Canadians" (2000) 1:5 *Policy Matters* at 13–16.

11 Seidle cites a study conducted by IPSOS-Reid in February 2001, which interviewed respondents on their attitudes towards—and knowledge of—the electoral system. F.L. Seidle, *Electoral System Reform in Canada: Objectives, Advocacy and Implications*

for Governance (Ottawa: Canadian Policy Research Networks Inc., 2002). The study found, among other things, that a significant number of Canadians do not understand first-past-the-post: "Fully 50 per cent of our respondents believe that a candidate must get a majority of all votes cast in a riding in order to win a Parliamentary seat. And 47 per cent believe that a political party must win a majority of all votes cast in order to form a government." D. Bricker and M. Redfern, "Canadian Perspectives on the Voting System" (2001) 22:6 *Policy Options* at 22.

12   Schwartz and Rettie, *supra* note 4 at 12.

13   Data compiled by the Inter-Parliamentary Union, and available on its website <http://www.ipu.org/wmn-e/classif.htm> (date accessed: 19 December 2003). A total of 181 countries were included in the data by the IPU; data were current as of May 2003.

14   D. Studlar, "Will Canada Seriously Consider Electoral Reform? Women and Aboriginals Should" in H. Milner ed., *Making Every Vote Count: Reassessing Canada's Electoral System* (Peterborough: Broadview Press, 1999) at 128.

15   T. Arseneau, "Electing Representative Legislatures: Lessons from New Zealand" in H. Milner ed., *Making Every Vote Count: Reassessing Canada's Electoral System* (Peterborough: Broadview Press, 1999) at 140.

16   Howe and Northrup, *supra* note 10 at 17.

17   Arseneau, *supra* note 15 at 144.

18   Howe and Northrup, *supra* note 10 at 19.

19   *Ibid.* at 20.

20   *Ibid.* at 19.

21   Schwartz and Rettie dissent from this conventional wisdom, arguing "there is no guarantee that PR will spontaneously generate more diverse candidates. [Also], the stigma of tokenism could reduce the credibility of [these] elected members." Schwartz and Rettie, *supra* note 4 at 51. It should be pointed out, however, that Arseneau's analysis of the New Zealand experience does highlight the modestly beneficial effect that a change in electoral system can have on the demographic representativeness of Parliament. See, T. Arseneau, "Electing Representative Legislatures: Lessons from New Zealand" in H. Milner ed., *Making Every Vote Count: Reassessing Canada's Electoral System* (Peterborough: Broadview Press, 1999).

22 Schwartz and Rettie, *supra* note 4 at 51; L. Young, *Electoral Systems and Representative Legislatures: Consideration of Alternative Electoral Systems* (Ottawa: Canadian Advisory Council on the Status of Women, 1994) at 6.

23 C. Taylor, cited in Royal Commission On Electoral Reform and Party Financing, *Final Report Volume I: Reforming Electoral Democracy* (Ottawa: Minister of Supply and Services, 1991) at 178.

24 Schwartz and Rettie, *supra* note 4 at 11.

25 *Ibid.* at 52.

26 P. Dunleavy, H. Margetts and S. Weir, *The Politico's Guide to Electoral Reform in Britain* (London: Politicos, 1998) at 15.

27 *Ibid.*

28 Schwartz and Rettie, *supra* note 4 at 13.

29 Blais, *supra* note 3 at 5.

30 *Ibid.* at 53.

31 J. Courtney, "Electoral Reform and Canada's Parties" in H. Milner ed., *Making Every Vote Count: Reassessing Canada's Electoral System* (Peterborough: Broadview Press, 1999) at 91; Schwartz and Rettie, *supra* note 4 at 53.

32 J. Simpson, *The Friendly Dictatorship* (Toronto: McClelland & Stewart, 2001); D. Savoie, *Governing from the Centre: The Concentration of Power in Canadian Politics* (Toronto: University of Toronto Press, 1999).

33 Blais, *supra* note 3 at 4.

34 Schwartz and Rettie, *supra* note 4 at 13.

35 *Ibid.* at 54

36 See, for example, Reynolds and Reilly, *supra* note 4.

37 Schwartz and Rettie, *supra* note 4 at 55.

38 See, for example, J. Rebick, "PR Can Help Solve Canada's Democracy Deficit" (July–August 2001) *Policy Options* at 16.

39 Schwartz and Rettie, *supra* note 4 at 55–56.

40 *Ibid.* at 39.

41 A. Cairns, "The Electoral System and the Party System in Canada, 1921–1965" (1968) 1 *Canadian Journal of Political Science* at 62. See, also, A. Cairns, "The Electoral System and the Party System in Canada, 1921-1965" in O. Kruhlak, R. Schultz and S. Pobihushchy eds., *The Canadian Political Process,* rev. ed. (Toronto: Holt, Rinehart and Winston, 1973).

42 See also, *The Report of the Royal Commission on the Economic Union and Development Prospects for Canada,* vol. 3. (Ottawa: Minister of Public Works and Government Services, 1985) at 84.

43 A. Cairns, "The Electoral System and the Party System in Canada, 1921–1965" in O. Kruhlak, R. Schultz and S. Pobihushchy eds., *The Canadian Political Process,* rev. ed. (Toronto: Holt, Rinehart and Winston, 1973) at 133.

44 *Ibid.* at 62.

45 *Ibid.* at 69–70.

46 *Ibid.*

47 Blais, *supra* note 3 at 5. (Emphasis original.)

Chapter 4 Electoral Options for Canada

Chapter 3 established ten criteria for assessing electoral systems, and used them to assess the first-past-the-post voting system. The results of that assessment suggest that it is time for Canada to explore different voting methods. From this stems a series of questions about possible options for Canada. What electoral systems fit with Canadians' democratic values? What are the strengths and limits of different alternatives? What level of proportionality should be adopted if Canadians were to add an element of proportionality to the existing voting system?

In the past 15 years, advocacy groups and political parties have put forward different suggestions that Canada's voters might consider adopting to improve our electoral system. Chapter 4 surveys these models, and discusses their strengths and limitations and how they relate to the ten criteria. It also explores the reasons why the Commission believes that a mixed member proportional system is the preferred option for Canada.

4.1 Balancing Competing Factors

The Commission's goal is to balance, to the extent possible, the benefits of introducing some element of proportionality into the existing system with the capacity to maintain accountable government, most notably as a direct link between elected politicians and their constituents. The Report explores the merits of different voting systems and suggests adding an element of proportionality could help achieve many of the criteria outlined in Section 3.3, such as improved demographic representation, a greater plurality of ideas and a more inclusive style of decision making. Despite concerns about the value of the relationship between Members of Parliament and their constituents, many citizens continue to desire some form of direct link with a constituency representative. Therefore, the Report examines different voting systems from the premise that constituencies should be kept to a reasonable size to maintain the relationship between Members of Parliament and constituents. This Report aims to add corrective features to our electoral rules that do not involve constitutional amendments, and hence do not deal with Senate reform. Finally, the Report also accepts the premise that there is little appetite for substantially increasing the size of the House of Commons to accommodate a new electoral system. Budgetary constraints make increasing the size of the House of Commons an unattractive option. These considerations, as well as our ten criteria, guided this exploration of different voting systems.

4.2 Majoritarian Systems

Majoritarian systems are designed to ensure the eventual winner is elected with a majority (more than 50 percent) of the vote. (See Section 2.2.1 for details.)

4.2.1 Two-round System

One type of majoritarian system is the two-round system, which has the following strengths.

- The two-round system attempts to ensure fairness in that the eventual winner is elected by a majority (more than 50 percent) of voters.

- It fosters geographic representation by retaining single-member constituencies.

- It attempts to address disregarded votes by giving voters a chance to change their selections between the first and second rounds of voting.

- It "encourages diverse interests to coalesce behind the successful candidates from the first round in the lead-up to the second round of voting, thus encouraging bargains and trade-offs between parties and candidates."[1] In this way, it attempts to encourage some consensual decision making.

The two-round system does have some serious drawbacks, however. It is the most costly of all the different types of electoral systems, placing tremendous strain on the electoral machinery of a country when the two rounds of voting are closely spaced. It is also highly disproportional and does not fare any better than the first-past-the-post system in translating votes into seats in the legislature.[2] Further, this system may allow "any candidate without broad support to win through to the second round on a small proportion of the vote, at the expense of a candidate with broad support."[3] For example, in a multi-party system, suppose there are two candidates— A and B—who are widely expected to proceed to the second round and this expectation is reported heavily in the media. In this scenario, it is conceivable that some voters might decide to wait until the second round to vote since the results seem to be a foregone conclusion. It is further conceivable that, as a result of not participating in the first round, candidate B does not make it through to the second round because a third candidate benefits from the lack of voter turnout and actually places second to candidate A. This could happen despite the fact that candidate B was the more popular candidate. Given these drawbacks, we believe that a two-round system should not be considered as a possible reform option for Canada.

4.2.2 Alternative Vote System

An alternative vote system is used to elect representatives to Australia's lower house, and was used at one time in British Columbia and in rural ridings in Alberta and Manitoba. It has a number of strengths.

- It is simple to use: the ballot is relatively uncomplicated.

- It fosters fairness since the winning candidate enjoys broad support.

- It retains the direct link between voter and representative (geographic representation).

- It encourages political moderation, since parties must seek the second preferences of voters who support other parties. They must, therefore, make "broadly-based, centrist appeals to all interests, and not focus on narrower sectarian or extremist issues."[4]

Among its disadvantages, it can be highly disproportional, although not as disproportional as most first-past-the-post or two-round systems. As well, there are still disregarded votes in this system. For example, many observers are concerned about the fact that the eventual winner of an alternative vote election is "likely to be pushed over the 50 percent line by the redistributed votes of the bottom ranked candidate. Leading parties may be encouraged to pander to the supporters of small parties, even if their views tend to be foolish or repressive."[5] In this respect, the second-choice votes of the rest of the parties are "wasted."[6] In light of current concerns, the alternative vote system is not sufficiently proportional to constitute a viable alternative to the first-past-the-post system.

4.3 Proportional Systems

4.3.1 Single Transferable Vote System

The single transferable vote system, which is currently used in Ireland, Malta, and to elect the Australian Senate, combines proportional representation with constituency politicians—in multi-member ridings.[7] The system has been used in Canada in urban, multi-member ridings in Manitoba (1927–57) and Alberta (1926–55). It has a number of advantages.

- Election results are reasonably proportional and, therefore, fair. For example, Ireland and Malta rank 15th and 20th, respectively, among 37 countries in terms of disproportionality. This places them well ahead of countries using plurality or majoritarian systems, but behind most of the countries using list-PR or mixed member proportional.[8]

- It allows voters greater choice in ranking candidates than a list-PR system (or mixed member proportional if it uses closed lists), and thus minimizes the influence of party "machines".

- It permits choice among parties and among individual candidates within parties.

- It retains the geographical or territorial link between voters and their representatives if the number of members per district is kept small.

The single transferable vote does have some disadvantages. First, the ballots used in single transferable vote systems and the process of tabulating votes can be somewhat complicated.[9] In the view of the United Kingdom's Independent Commission on the Voting System, these systems provide voters with *too much* choice: the ballot resembles "a caricature of an over-zealous American breakfast waiter going on posing an indefinite number of unwanted options, ... [which] becomes both an exasperation and an incitement to the giving of random answers."[10] Second, the vote counting procedure for single transferable vote is complex[11] and potentially time-consuming.[12] Third, this system can foster intra-party competition and fragmentation, thereby discouraging consensual decision making.[13]

Finally, the single transferable vote system, because of its use of multi-member constituencies (geographic representation), represents a significant departure from the one-member–one-riding principle seemingly cherished in the Anglo-American democracies, including Canada. For example, in a province such as Ontario, to accommodate a single transferable vote system, it is conceivable that the number of constituencies would have to be reduced from the current total of 103 to somewhere in the neighbourhood of 20 to 25. In the end, the single transferable vote has several strengths, including its ability to produce proportional governments, making it a promising alternative to the first-past-the-post system. However, the potential limitations, particularly the departure from the constituent–Member of Parliament principle, make it a difficult option to pursue for Canada *at this time*.

4.3.2 List-PR System

Many countries in Western Europe have employed a list-PR system. It has the following advantages.

- It offers proportionality of seats to votes (in other words, fair representation of parties).

- It can promote demographic representation, to ensure that the legislature does indeed closely mirror the demographic profile of the nation.

- There are no or few disregarded votes, depending on district magnitude and thresholds.

- It makes power-sharing between parties and interest groups more visible. By "including all interests in parliament, [this system] offers a better hope that decisions are taken in the public eye, and by a more inclusive cross-section of the society."[14]

- Countries with list-PR systems tend to have a consensual style of policy making, as opposed to the adversarial and often combative politics characteristic of majoritarian and plurality systems.

Although it provides a strong element of proportionality, a list-PR system represents a significant departure from our Parliamentary tradition. An inevitable consequence of such a reform, even if the number of members elected per riding were relatively small (five or six), would be attenuation of the geographic representation link between voters in a given territory and their representatives. As well, this kind of system could increase the role of party organizations in determining who gets elected because they determine placement on the party lists. However, as this Report notes below, using lists in which voters select their preferred candidates could ameliorate this feature.[15]

For these reasons, the list-PR system is also excluded from the possible options for electoral reform in Canada, leaving essentially only one further alternative to explore: a mixed system.

4.4 Mixed Electoral Systems

Most nations that have reformed their electoral systems in the past decade have opted for some version of a mixed or parallel system. These systems are thought to combine the "best of both worlds": the accountability and geographic representation that is one of the strengths of first-past-the-post and other plurality formulas, along with the demographic representativeness and fairness of proportional representation systems.[16] There are many varieties of mixed or hybrid electoral systems, but they all share one defining characteristic: in each, a portion of the seats in parliament are assigned on the basis of some plurality method, usually first-past-the-post[17] in single-member constituencies, and the remaining seats are determined by a party's share of the popular vote (regionally or nationally). In such systems, voters usually have two votes, one for a given candidate in a riding, and another for a party list.

Section 4.4 examines two different types of mixed electoral systems as possible alternatives to Canada's first-past-the-post system: mixed member majoritarian and mixed member proportional. To highlight how these different electoral systems might function in the Canadian context, we constructed a series of examples using results from previous federal elections. However, in doing so we must inject a word of caution: it is certain that voter calculations and behaviour would change with the implementation of a new electoral system, especially one that increased voter choice by providing two options (candidate vote, party vote) on the ballot. For example, with a mixed member system, a voter may decide to "split" his or her vote by voting at the constituency level for a member of one party, and for a different party at the provincial or regional level. Furthermore, a different system would also produce much different electoral campaign strategies. First-past-the-post tends to encourage regionally concentrated campaigns (focusing on winnable ridings), compared to mixed member proportional systems which encourage parties to seek broad-based or national support.[18] Different campaign strategies could potentially alter voter behaviour at the ballot box. Finally, other parties not represented in the 2000 federal election results could become viable choices under a different voting system. For example, many voters might have voted for the Green Party if the system in use at the time awarded seats on a more proportional basis. Therefore, illustrating how different voting systems *might* work using previous election results can only provide some understanding of how mixed electoral systems might work. They do not necessarily indicate what the results *would have been* or *would be* under a different system.

Throughout the examples each province and territory is used as the basis for assigning list or compensatory seats. Choices for determining compensatory seats are constrained by Canada's geography and by its constitution.[19] Theoretically, it would be possible to create five or six regions in Canada corresponding to "natural" geographic divisions: the Atlantic provinces, Quebec, Ontario, the prairie provinces and British Columbia.[20] However, there is at least a possibility that the creation of such supra-provincial districts might require a constitutional amendment. The so-called Senate clause stipulates that every province has a right to "a number of members in the House of Commons not less than the number of Senators by which the province is entitled to be represented …"[21] If, for example, the Atlantic region were assigned 20 single-seat constituencies and 12 compensatory list seats, this would mean that Prince Edward Island would have its number of single-seat constituencies reduced from four to one or two. This *might* violate the Senate clause, even if Prince Edward Island were to be assigned two or three of the regional compensatory seats. This is because these regional seats would be determined by means of aggregate votes from all four provinces, and it is possible that the results from Prince Edward Island might not factor into the regional results, i.e., the weight of the results from outside of Prince Edward Island would be greater than results from inside the province.

There would also be a number of questions about how to assign which compensatory seats to which province if supra-provincial regions were created. For example, would the representatives in regional seats in Prince Edward Island have to come from that province? What happens if the regional seat in Prince Edward Island is awarded to a party with no candidates in that province? While there are merits to establishing regional lists, the constitutional concerns (including having to amend the constitution to accommodate extra-provincial compensation seats) mean that establishing compensation lists within existing provinces and territories would be more appropriate.

The proposed ratio of two-thirds first-past-the-post and one-third proportionality is intended to achieve the goal outlined at the beginning of the Chapter. First, the size of the House of Commons is kept at 301 seats (308 after the next redistribution), since expanding the number of seats should be avoided, *unless* additional seats are required to represent either Aboriginal people or the territories. Second, geographic representation (the Member of Parliament–constituent link) is maintained. Constituencies are kept at a reasonable size; something that is attainable with an element of proportionality within the range of one-third of the seats in the House of Commons.

4.4.1   Mixed Member Majoritarian System

The mixed member majoritarian system considered here is similar to the one adopted in Japan in 1994. In this system, the two tiers of seats, each determined by its own electoral formula, are independent of each other, that is, no attempt is made to use the party-list vote or proportional component to compensate for distortions in the constituency vote. Depending on how they are designed, these systems can minimize the likelihood of minority or coalition government.

The Pepin-Robarts Report proposed a mixed member majoritarian system for Canada. It recommended that the existing House of Commons (which then had 282 members) be expanded by 60 members (about an 18 percent increase). Seats would be "awarded to parties on the basis of percentages of the popular vote."[22] In essence, this proposal would have balanced regional disparities in the vote, but it would not have had much of an impact on the disproportionality of seats to votes.[23] The Liberals would have taken 51 percent of the seats in the expanded House of Commons, as opposed to the 52 percent that they actually won with their 44 percent of the vote. The authors of the report concluded that this system would "make representation more proportionate, would ... [produce] a more broadly based representation within each party in the Commons, but would not ... significantly [increase] the incidence of minority governments."[24]

Table 7 and figure 6 present the actual election results from the 2000 federal elections, broken down by province and party. Table 8 presents the simulated results using a mixed member majoritarian formula in which two-thirds of the seats are elected on the basis of first-past-the-post and the remaining one-third are drawn from provincial party lists. Each province constitutes a single region with anywhere from 1 (Prince Edward Island) to 34 (Ontario) list seats. For this illustration, we simply assume that each party would have won the same *proportion* of the first-past-the-post seats under the mixed formula as they did. Since the Liberals won 172 of the 301 seats, this translates into 116 seats in the plurality component of our model.[25]

Table 7   Seats won by each party, by province, 2000 federal election

	LIB	CA	PC	BQ	NDP	Totals
Nfld. and Lab.	5	0	2	0	0	7
P.E.I.	4	0	0	0	0	4
N.S.	4	0	4	0	3	11
N.B.	6	0	3	0	1	10
Que.	36	0	1	38	0	75
Ont.	100	2	0	0	1	103
Man.	5	4	1	0	4	14
Sask.	2	10	0	0	2	14
Alta.	2	23	1	0	0	26
B.C.	5	27	0	0	2	34
Y.T.	1	0	0	0	0	1
N.W.T.	1	0	0	0	0	1
Nun.	1	0	0	0	0	1
Total	172	66	12	38	13	301

Figure 6 Percentage of current seats, 2000 federal election

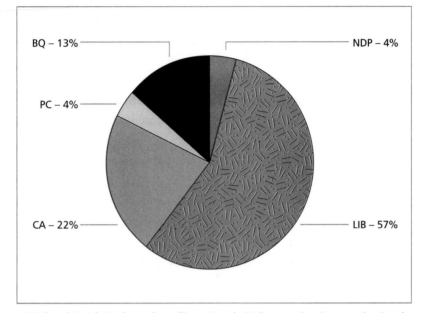

LIB (Liberal Party); CA (Canadian Alliance Party); PC (Progressive Conservative Party); BQ (Bloc Qébécois Party); NDP (New Democratic Party).

As a result, the size of the average constituency in our model would increase by approximately one-third. The largest ridings in the country (Brampton West–Mississauga in Ontario and Surrey Central in British Colimbia) which at present have populations of more than 130,000, would grow to about 173,000. While this creates larger ridings, the impact of this expansion could be lessened somewhat by the fact that the new regional Members of Parliament may have constituency duties as well, just as they do in New Zealand and Scotland.[26]

In addition, to ensure adequate representation of Nunavut, Northwest Territories, and Yukon, one additional list seat would be assigned per territory. In the territories the proportional increase in the number of list seats would be greater than in the provinces. However, since the territories have only one constituency seat each under the existing first-past-the-post system, the additional seats were necessary to include the territories in the compensatory (list) system and to better represent this part of the country in the House of Commons (something that a new voting system would attempt to accomplish in the provinces). Therefore, list seats for the territories are automatic and do not factor in to the overall compensation formula. This adds 3 additional seats (1 for each territory), for a total of 304 seats in the House of Commons, which would become 311 after the next redistribution.

The data in table 8 and figure 7 show that the proposed mixed member majoritarian system would have increased the fairness of the election results, that is reduced disproportionality, but only slightly. The Liberals would have won 161 seats (53 percent of the total) as opposed to the 172 (or 57 percent) that they actually took. This figure is more in line with their share of the popular vote in 2000 (41 percent), but nevertheless still represents a considerable electoral bonus. The impact of the mixed member majoritarian formula on results in the Atlantic provinces and in the west would have been negligible. However, the Canadian Alliance Party would have picked up a list seat in Quebec and 8 list seats in Ontario, while the

Figure 7 Illustrated results (mixed member majoritarian) percentage of seats

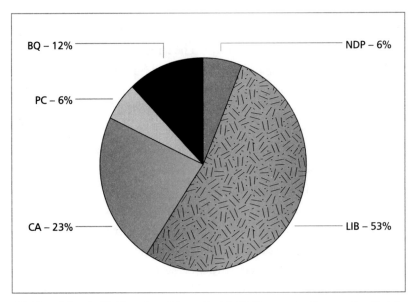

LIB (Liberal Party); CA (Canadian Alliance Party); PC (Progressive Conservative Party); BQ (Bloc Québécois Party); NDP (New Democratic Party).

Table 8 Simulated 2000 federal election results calculated using a mixed member majoritarian system, assigning constituency seats (CS) and list seats (LS)

	LIB		CA		PC		BQ		NDP		Totals	
	CS	LS	CS	LS	CS	LS	CS	LS	CS	LS	CS	LS
Nfld. and Lab.	4	1			1	1					5	2
P.E.I.	3	1									3	1
N.S.	3	2			2	1			2	1	7	4
N.B.	4	2			2	1			1		7	3
Que.	24	12		1	1	1	25	11			50	25
Ont.	67	18	1	8		5			1	3	69	34
Man.	3	2	3	2	1				2	1	9	5
Sask.	1	1	7	3					1	1	9	5
Alta.	1	2	15	6	1	1					17	9
B.C.	3	3	18	7		1			1		22	12
Y.T.	1									1	1	1*
N.W.T.	1									1	1	1*
Nun.	1	1									1	1*
Seat totals by type and party	116 +	45	44 +	27	8 +	11	25 +	11	8 +	9	201 +	103
Total Seats by Party	161		71		19		36		17		304	

* One list seat is automatically awarded to each territory to ensure greater inclusion of this region of the country in the system of democratic governance.

Progressive Conservative Party would have picked up 5 list seats in Ontario. In the end, it is difficult to disagree with the conclusion of the New Zealand Royal Commission on the Electoral System that this kind of electoral formula is more of a palliative than a substantive reform, even if it does address one of the dysfunctional aspects of our first-past-the-post system. Its principal benefit is that the legislative caucuses of the various parties, especially the governing party, would be more regionally representative. However, since it only partially addresses the issue of disproportionality, this model does not make it an attractive option in terms of fairness to parties.

4.4.2 Mixed Member Proportional System

An alternative type of mixed system is one in which the two components, or tiers, are linked: "Whereas MMM [mixed member majoritarian] systems add seats from the list tier in parallel, *even for parties that are already over-represented in the [plurality] tier*, systems with compensatory seat linkage provide list seats to compensate parties that are under-represented" in the first-past-the-post results.[27] The election results in such systems, designated mixed member proportional, are usually highly proportional and fair.[28] Examples of these systems can be found in Germany, Scotland, and New Zealand. In these countries, voters are given two votes: one for their constituency representative, and one for a party. It is the party vote that is primary:[29] a party's share of the seats in parliament is determined by the party vote, and the number of constituency seats it wins is then *subtracted* from this total. The remaining seats are filled from party lists.

4.4.3 Germany's Mixed Member Proportional System

In Germany, 50 percent of the seats in the Bundestag are based on constituency elections and the other 50 percent are list seats. In New Zealand, 58 percent of the seats are single-member constituencies elected by means of first-past-the-post, and the remaining 42 percent are list seats. In the Scottish Parliament, which consists of 129 members, 73 (57 percent) are elected in constituencies by means of first-past-the-post, and the remaining 56 (43 percent) are awarded to regional lists.[30]

Table 9 and figure 8 display the results of the 2000 federal election under a German-style mixed member proportional formula, with 60 percent of the seats determined by first-past-the-post and the remainder by provincial party lists.[31] This second model assumes that there is a 5 percent threshold (or one constituency victory) that a party must surpass to qualify for the list seats. However, in our model, this threshold is set at the provincial level, rather than nationally, as in Germany.[32] In the simulated results, this threshold came into play only once: the New Democratic Party was deprived of a list seat that it would have won in Quebec had it passed the 5 percent provincial hurdle.

The second mixed member model produces the most proportionate results of the three models. The Liberals would have won 137 seats (44.4 percent of the total) with 40.8 percent of the popular vote (figures for the other parties are contained in table 11). Thus either a minority or a coalition government would have been necessary after the election, which would have required consensus building

Figure 8 Illustrated results (mixed member proportional—
Germany) percentage of seats

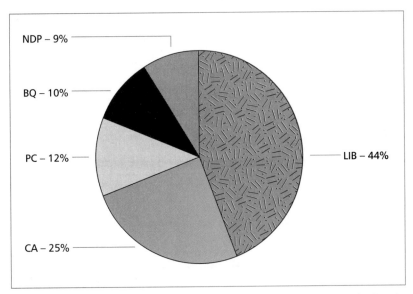

NDP – 9%

BQ – 10%

PC – 12%

LIB – 44%

CA – 25%

LIB (Liberal Party); CA (Canadian Alliance Party); PC (Progressive Conservative Party); BQ (Bloc Québécois Party); NDP (New Democratic Party).

Table 9 Simulated 2000 federal election results calculated using a mixed member proportional system (German Model), assigning constituency seats (CS) and list seats (LS)

	LIB		CA		PC		BQ		NDP		Totals	
	CS	LS	CS	LS	CS	LS	CS	LS	CS	LS	CS	LS
Nfld. and Lab.	3				1	2				1	4	3
P.E.I.	1	1				2					1	3
N.S.	3	1		1	2	1			2	1	7	4
N.B.	3	2		1	2	1			1		6	4
Que.	21	14		4	1	3	23	9			45	30
Ont.	60		1	24		15			1	7	62	46
Man.	3	2	2	2	1	1			2	1	8	6
Sask.	1	2	6	1					1	3	8	6
Alta.	1	5	14	2	1	2				1	16	10
B.C.	3	7	16	2		2			1	3	20	14
Y.T.	1									1	1	1*
N.W.T.	1									1	1	1*
Nun.	1	1									1	1*
Seat totals by type and party	102	+ 35	39	+ 37	8	+ 29	23	+ 9	8	+ 19	180	+ 129
Total seats by party	137		76		37		32		27		309	

* One list seat is automatically awarded to each territory to ensure greater inclusion of this region of the country in the system of democratic governance.

and inclusive decision making. The Liberal caucus would also have been more regionally representative: only 60 of its 137 members would have come from Ontario (44 percent, as opposed to the actual 58 percent), and the party would have gained list members in British Columbia and Alberta.

There is, however, one feature of the German system that renders it inappropriate for implementation in Canada, and this is readily apparent in the results contained in table 9. With a 60/40 split between constituencies and list seats, Ontario should have 62 first-past-the-post seats and 41 list seats, for a total of 103 seats. Why then are there 5 extra list seats (46 instead of 41)? In the German mixed member proportional system, it is quite possible for a party to win many more constituencies than the total number of seats to which its share of the party vote entitles it.[33] This would have occurred in Ontario in every election since 1993.[34] There are different ways to deal with this surplus of seats, at least in theory. For example, one could subtract list seats from the Liberals' totals in other provinces—a politically risky move at best, and one that undercuts one of the principal virtues of a mixed system, namely its ability to produce more regionally representative party caucuses.[35]

The solution adopted in the German system for dealing with such situations appears to be the optimal one: parties are allowed to keep their extra seats (labeled *Überhangmandate*, or overhang seats) and the size of the legislature increases for that particular mandate.[36] Although this is probably the best way of dealing with this feature of German-style mixed member proportional voting, it is unlikely to gain widespread acceptance among Canadians. Furthermore, such a solution could raise constitutional issues, since a province might receive a sufficient number of overhang seats to make its share of the seats in the House of Commons no longer proportionate to its population. Section 42(1)(a) of the *Constitution Act, 1982*,[37] stipulates that any change in this principle of proportionate representation in Parliament would require the approval of at least two-thirds of the provinces that have at least 50 percent of the country's population.[38]

4.4.4 Scotland's Mixed Member Proportional System

Because of this feature of the German model, the mixed member proportional version adopted by the Scottish Parliament is more suitable for a country like Canada. Devolution in Great Britain led to the creation of sub-national legislatures in Scotland and Wales. Both implemented versions of mixed member proportional systems, which were first used in elections in 1999. Voters in each region are given two votes, one for a candidate in a single-member constituency, the other for a party list representing a given region (corresponding to the constituencies for elections to the European Parliament). The Scottish Parliament has 129 members, 73 (57 percent) elected in single-member constituencies and 56 (43 percent) in 8 multi-member regional ridings.

The distribution of regional seats in Scotland and Wales is calculated as follows: the total number of votes cast for a party list is divided by the number of constituencies won by that party in the region, plus one.[39] This method yields quite proportional results, although they are not perfectly proportional. In the 1999 Scottish elections, for instance, the Labour Party received just fewer than 34 percent of the regional list vote, but won 43 percent of the total seats in Parliament. The Scottish National Party (SNP) took 27 percent of the vote and 27 percent of the seats, while the Conservatives won 15 percent of the vote and 14 percent of the seats. The Green Party, which did not contest a single constituency election, nonetheless won one regional seat with its 3.6 percent of the party list vote.

Table 10 and figure 9 display the results of our simulation of the 2000 federal election using a Scottish-style mixed member proportional formula.[40] The first decision to make in adapting this system to Canada's circumstances involves the split between first-past-the-post and proportional representation seats. There is considerable variation in the proportion of seats allotted to each tier in those countries that have adopted mixed member proportional electoral systems. They range from a low of 25 percent proportional representation seats in Italy's lower house to 50 percent in Germany.

In this demonstration model, a figure of 33 percent (one-third) was chosen for two reasons. First, this split yields fair and highly

Table 10 Simulated 2000 federal election results calculated using a mixed member proportional system (Scottish Model), assigning constituency seats (CS) and list seats (LS)

	LIB		CA		PC		BQ		NDP		Totals	
	CS	LS	CS	LS	CS	LS	CS	LS	CS	LS	CS	LS
Nfld. and Lab.	3				1	2				1	4	3
P.E.I.	1	1				2					1	3
N.S.	3	1		1	2	1			2	1	7	4
N.B.	3	2		1	2	1			1		6	4
Que. 1**	11	6		3	1	1	15	3			27	13
Que. 2**	13	5		1		2	10	4			23	12
Ont. 1**	23		1	6		3				2	24	11
Ont. 2**	22			8		4			1		23	12
Ont. 3**	22			5		4				2	22	11
Man.	3	2	3	1	1	1			2	1	9	5
Sask.	1	2	7						1	3	9	5
Alta.	1	5	15	1	1	2				1	17	9
B.C.	3	7	18			2			1	3	22	12
Y.T.	1									1	1	1*
N.W.T	1	1									1	1*
Nun.	1									1	1	1*
Seat totals by type and party	112	+ 32	44	+ 27	8	+ 25	25	+ 7	8	+ 16	197	+ 107
Total seats by party	144		71		33		32		24		304	

* One list seat is automatically awarded to each territory to ensure greater inclusion of this region of the country in the system of democratic governance.

** Because of the large populations in Quebec and Ontario, regions within each province were created to prevent the provincial lists from being too large. See Appendix A for a description of the regions within Quebec and Ontario.

proportional results, as the data in table 10 indicate. Some observers have demonstrated that deviations from proportionality in most first-past-the-post electoral systems are usually no more than 25 percent or 30 percent, and thus if the compensatory seats number around one-quarter to one-third of the total, the overall results will be very close to proportional.[41] Second, the ceiling for compensatory seats at 33 percent also allows us to meet the criteria for geographic representation by keeping the constituencies to a reasonable size. Because the number of single-member ridings in our model is reduced by one-third, their average size will automatically grow by a similar figure, creating some constituencies with populations upwards of 175,000. This is certainly not out of line with the size of constituencies in some European countries, but it does represent a significant departure from the status quo in Canada.

The results displayed in table 10 and figure 9 are fair and relatively proportional, although the Liberals do receive a bonus of approximately 7 percent (the figure by which their share of the seats

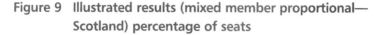

Figure 9   Illustrated results (mixed member proportional—
Scotland) percentage of seats

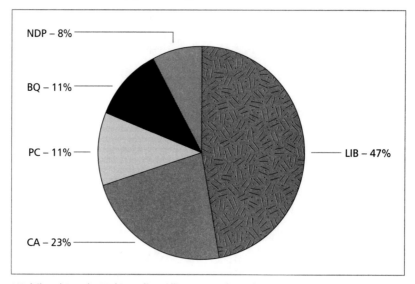

NDP – 8%

BQ – 11%

PC – 11%

LIB – 47%

CA – 23%

LIB (Liberal Party); CA (Canadian Alliance Party); PC (Progressive Conservative Party); BQ (Bloc Québécois Party); NDP (New Democratic Party).

Determining the distribution of provincial and territorial list seats (LS) using the "Scottish Formula" (example from 2000 federal election).

Alberta: 17 Constituency Seats plus 9 List Seats

	CA	LIB	PC	NDP	LS to:
N = Provincial Votes	739,514	263,008	169,093	68,363	
N= Constituencies Won	15	1	1	0	
Divisor 1 (constituency seats +1)	16	2	2	1	
Result 1	46,219.63	**131,504**	84,546.5	68,363	LIB
Divisor 2	16	2+1 (3)	2	1	
Result 2	46,219.63	**87,669.33**	84,546.5	68,363	LIB
Divisor 3	16	3+1 (4)	2	1	
Result 3	46,219.63	65,752	**84,564.3**	68,363	PC
Divisor 4	16	4	2+1 (3)	1	
Result 4	46,219.63	65,752	56,364.33	**68,363**	NDP
Divisor 5	16	4	3	1+1 (2)	
Result 5	46,219.63	**65,752**	56,364.33	34,181.5	LIB
Divisor 6	16	4+1 (5)	3	2	
Result 6	46,219.63	52,601.6	**56,364.33**	34,181.5	PC
Divisor 7	16	5	3+1 (4)	2	
Result 7	46,219.63	**52,601.6**	42,273.25	34,181.5	LIB
Divisor 8	16	5+1 (6)	4	2	
Result 8	**46,219.63**	43,834.67	42,273.25	34,181.5	CA
Divisor 9	16+1 (17)	6	4	2	
Result 9	43,500.82	**43,834.67**	42,273.25	34,181.5	LIB
Total List Seats	1	5	2	1	

LIB wins 23% of seats with 21% of provincial vote
CA wins 62% of seats with 59% of vote
NDP wins 4% of seats with 5% of vote
PC wins 12% of seats with 14% of vote

An example of the calculations required to distribute Canadian provincial and territorial list seats, taken from our illustration of the 2000 federal election using the Scottish model, can be found above. There are a total of 26 seats to be awarded—17 constituency seats and 9 list seats (using Alberta as an example). To determine the allocation of list seats, begin by totaling the provincial votes for each party. In this instance, the Canadian Alliance Party (CA) received 739,514 provincial votes, the Liberal Party (LIB) 263,008, the Progressive Conservative Party (PC) 169,093 and the New Democratic Party (NDP) 68,363. Following this, divide the number of provincial votes by the number of constituency seats each party won in the first-past-the-post portion of the ballot, plus one. The "plus one" is to ensure that parties that did not win a constituency seat still have an opportunity to receive a list seat. For example, the CA won 15 constituency seats. Add 1 to this for a divisor of 16. Similarly, the NDP won 0 constituency seats, so that party's divisor would be 1. The result of dividing the provincial votes by the constituency seats, plus 1, reveals that the LIB received the highest provincial figure of 131,504, which is the party's provincial vote divided by 2. (This result is in bold in the row marked Result 1.) The LIB would therefore receive the first list seat in Alberta.

Repeat the process to determine which party receives the second list seat. Once again, divide the provincial votes for each party by the number of their constituency seats, plus one. The only difference this time is that the party that received the last list seat (in this case, the LIB) would have another 1 added to their divisor, which means they would now have a divisor of 3 (otherwise all of the division results would remain the same). As a result, the LIB provincial figure is now 87,669.33. They still have the highest provincial figure and therefore receive the second list seat. (This result is in bold in the row marked Result 2.) Repeat the process again to determine which party receives the third list seat. The LIB would have another 1 added to their divisor since they received the second list seat, for a divisor of 4. In this instance we can see the LIB provincial figure is now

65,752—the figure in the row marked Result 3, under LIB. The LIB no longer has the highest provincial figure; this time it is the PC, with a figure of 84,564.3—the figure in the row marked Result 3, under PC. The PC therefore receives the third list seat. Repeat the process again to determine which party would receive the fourth list seat. This time the PC would have 1 added to their divisor since they received the third list seat.

The calculation process continues until all list seats are awarded. In the end, we can see that each party was compensated by at least one seat (the column marked "LS to" indicates which party received each of the compensation seats). In addition, the final results are relatively proportional and therefore fair to each of the parties. The LIB receives 23 percent of the seats with 21 percent of the provincial vote; the CA 62 percent of the seats with 59 percent of the vote; the PC 12 percent of the seats with 14 percent of the votes; and the NDP 4 percent of the seats with 5 percent of the vote.

exceeds their share of the votes), mostly thanks to their sweep of virtually all of the constituency races in Ontario. For the other four parties, the discrepancy between vote shares and seat shares is around 1 percent (see table 11). The Scottish model eliminates the problem of overhang seats and it results in more balanced representation for all of the parties in the various regions of the country. The Canadian Alliance would have picked up 4 list seats in Quebec and 19 in Ontario, while the Liberals would have gained 11 list seats in Quebec and 5 and 7 in Alberta and British Columbia, respectively. The Progressive Conservative Party would have gained 5 list seats in the Atlantic provinces, 3 in Quebec and 11 in Ontario, and the New Democratic Party would have won an additional 4 seats in Ontario and 8 in the western provinces.

A Scottish-inspired mixed member proportional system would do a much better job of being fair and making every vote count than our

Table 11 Disproportionality in election results under different electoral formulas, 2000 federal election

		FPTP Actual Results		MMM Japanese Model		MMP1 German Model		MMP2 Scottish Model	
	%votes	%seats	diff.*	%seats	diff.*	%seats	diff.*	%seats	diff.*
LIB	40.8	57.1	16.3	52.1	11.3	44.4	3.6	47.4	6.6
CA	25.5	21.9	-3.6	23.3	-2.2	24.6	-0.9	23.3	-2.2
PC	12.2	4.0	-8.2	6.3	-5.9	12.0	-0.2	10.9	-1.3
NDP	8.5	4.3	-4.2	5.6	-2.9	8.7	0.2	7.9	-0.6
BQ	10.7	12.6	1.9	11.8	1.1	10.4	-0.3	10.5	-0.2
Total Distortion**		34.2		23.4		5.2		10.9	

*difference/distortion = % seats – % votes
**sum of absolute values of all differences from proportionality
FPTP (first-past-the-post); MMM (mixed member majoritarian); MMP1 (mixed member proportional—German model); MMP2 (mixed member proportional—Scottish Model).

"In the preceding discussion of the respective strengths and weaknesses of MMP, STV and plurality, we have endeavoured to present a fair appraisal. Of the 2 proportional systems, MMP and STV, it is our view that for New Zealand MMP is clearly superior. It is fairer to supporters of significant *political parties* and likely to provide more *effective representation* of *Maori* and other *minority* and *special interest groups*. It is likely to provide a more *effective Parliament* and also has advantages in terms of *voter participation* and *legitimacy*."

New Zealand, Royal Commission on the Electoral System, *Towards a Better Democracy* (Wellington: Government Printer, 1986) at 63. (Emphasis added.)

---

current system. It would reduce the regional imbalances in the legislative caucuses of all the major parties. It would promote fairness, and encourage demographic representation by ensuring the entry of new voices into the legislature, particularly those of currently under-represented groups and encourage a plurality of ideas in the system of governance. In turn, it would help to energize and invigorate this country's parliamentary democracy. For these reasons, among others presented here, the Commission makes the following principal recommendations:

Recommendation 1

The Law Commission of Canada recommends adding an element of proportionality to Canada's electoral system.

Recommendation 2

The Law Commission of Canada recommends that Canada adopt a mixed member proportional electoral system.

One of the most important features of the mixed member proportional system used in New Zealand, Germany, Scotland, and Wales is that it is a two-vote system of proportional representation. Canadians need to understand the implications of this.[42] Voters are allowed to ticket-split, that is, vote for a candidate of one party in their riding, and for another party on the proportional representation portion of the ballot (See figure 10 for an example of a possible mixed member proportional ballot). This feature helps to alleviate the disregarded vote phenomenon that is characteristic of the first-past-the-post system. According to the Jenkins Report, it gives voters maximum choice and flexibility: it frees them "from the prison of having to suffer an unwanted candidate for the constituency in order to get a desired government."[43] Interestingly, in the first mixed member proportional election held in New Zealand in 1996, 37 percent of voters split their ticket—"a high level by international standards. This suggests 'that New Zealanders clearly relished the opportunity ... to distinguish between two very different propositions formerly concealed when voting under first-past-the-post.'"[44]

Figure 10 Mock ballot for a mixed member proportional system (Scottish model) for Canada[45]

Constituency Vote This vote will help to decide the constituency Member of Parliament for your riding. Vote by placing an X beside the candidate of your choice.		Party/Provincial-Territorial Vote This vote will help to decide the total number of seats for each party in your Province or Territory. You may vote either for one party or, if you wish, for one of the listed candidates. A vote for a listed candidate will also be counted as a vote for that candidate's party.	
	Vote for one candidate ONLY	**Either** Put an X against the party of your choice	**Or** Put an X against the candidate of your choice
Candidate A Red Party		❏ Red Party **OR**	❏ Gilles Purple ❏ Emily Orange ❏ Ivan Pink
Candidate B White Party		❏ White Party **OR**	❏ Candidate name ❏ Candidate name ❏ Candidate name
Candidate C Blue Party		❏ Blue Party **OR**	❏ Candidate name ❏ Candidate name ❏ Candidate name
Candidate D Green Party		❏ Green Party **OR**	❏ Candidate name ❏ Candidate name ❏ Candidate name

Recommendation 3

A mixed member proportional system should be based on giving voters TWO votes: one for a constituency representative and one for a party list. The party vote should determine who is to be elected from provincial and territorial lists as drawn up by the parties before the election.

Table 12 Comparative assessment of electoral systems

Criteria	FPTP	AV – TRS	AV	STV	List- PR	MMM	MMP – German Model	MMP – Scottish Model
1. Representation of Parties		✔	✔	✔	✔		✔	✔
2. Demographic Representation				✔	✔		✔	✔
3. Geographic Representation	✔	✔	✔			✔	✔	✔
4. Diversity of Ideas				✔	✔		✔	✔
5. Effective Government	✔	✔	✔				✔	✔
6. Accountable Government	✔	✔	✔	✔		✔	✔	✔
7. Effective Opposition							✔	✔
8. Valuing Votes		✔	✔	✔	✔	✔	✔	✔
9. Regional Balance						✔	✔	✔
10. Inclusive Decisions					✔		✔	✔

Note: A ✔ represents strengths or potential strength. The absence of a ✔ does not suggest a total lack of this criterion, but rather our analysis indicates that it is not immediately evident if this criteria could be met in the Canadian context.

As stated earlier, a reformed electoral system for Canada should not require a significant expansion of the membership of the House of Commons, although additional seats for the territories should be included in the new system. In addition, the share of proportional representation list seats in the House of Commons ought to be at least one-quarter, and preferably a third of the total, if we wish to compensate for the distortions in the first-past-the-post component.

This leads to the next recommendation:

Recommendation 4

Two-thirds of the members of the House of Commons should be elected in constituency races using the first-past-the-post method, and the remaining one-third should be elected from provincial or territorial party lists. In addition, one list seat each should be allotted to Nunavut, Northwest Territories, and Yukon.

4.5 Diversity and Representation

4.5.1 Open Versus Closed Lists

Several important questions remain to be addressed when designing a mixed member proportional electoral system for Canada. First, how should candidates be elected from provincial or territorial lists? Should list seats be assigned on the basis of closed or open party lists, or a method that combines aspects of both? In most proportional representation systems, each party draws up a list of rank-ordered candidates for a given area. If, for example, the Blue Party is running for election in an eight-seat district with 1000 voters and it receives 500 votes (50 percent of the total), the top four candidates on its list would be elected. If it is a closed-list system, then voters do not have any opportunity to alter the order in which the candidates on the list are to be elected; the list is, in essence, a party slate. Numerous critics of this procedure have pointed out that it gives an enormous advantage to party elites, who can place themselves at the top of the lists. At the same time, however, closed lists can allow party officials to place members of under-represented groups, such as women and ethnic or religious minorities, at the top of the lists.

Despite the advantages of closed lists as vehicles for electoral affirmative action, they have been unpopular with voters. Research published in New Zealand in 2000 noted that party elites in that country overwhelmingly favoured closed lists. However, a solid majority of voters supported open lists and believed that it was up to the electorate to decide the order of election from the party list.[46]

Based on the feedback received during our consultation process, many Canadian voters would also most likely desire the flexibility of open lists in a mixed member proportional system. In essence, allowing voters to choose a candidate from the list provides voters with the ability to select a specific individual and hold them accountable for their actions should they be elected.

Having an open list gives voters the chance to endorse one or more candidates on the party list, which helps avoid the perception of disregarded votes. If a candidate receives enough votes on this open ballot, he or she might be able to leapfrog over other candidates ranked higher on the list and thus be elected. Research in a number of countries seems to indicate that this process alters the allocation of a small proportion of seats, in part because political parties chose their lists carefully so that voters decide against altering the party's list, and because successfully changing the party-determined order of list candidates requires considerable coordination among voters and individual candidates.[47]

While open lists may well foster greater voter choice, they are not without drawbacks. First, they encourage factionalism and intra-party competition. These were such prominent features of the open ballots previously employed in Italy that they led to a reform of the ballot in the early 1990s.[48] In the United Kingdom, a Labour Member of Parliament advocated the use of closed lists for elections to the European Parliament, stating that supporters of open lists "are calling for ... open warfare between all seven candidates on the same list as they fight each other to make sure they get the biggest possible personal vote."[49] Second, open lists are not as effective in promoting the candidacy and successful election of women, unless quotas are established guaranteeing women a certain percentage of winnable positions.[50]

These contradictory effects of open and closed lists clearly require exploring a compromise solution for the type of ballot to be included in any future reform of our electoral system. The Jenkins Commission has advocated what some have called a flexible list, one that gives voters the option of either endorsing the party slate on the list portion of the ballot or of indicating a preference for one particular candidate.[51] Our mock ballot for a mixed member proportional system illustrates a flexible voting method (See figure 10). In this scenario, after determining the number of list or compensation seats that a party is entitled to, the next question is which candidate or candidates should be awarded the additional seats. Should it be the list candidate identified by the party ranking, or an individual within the list, as selected by voters? To answer this, we can turn to other jurisdictions to look at how they award list seats within a flexible-type system.

In Sweden, for example, each party develops a list of ranked-ordered candidates. If a party submits a list of 15 candidates, ranked 1 to 15, and wins 10 seats in the election, then seats would be allocated to the top 10 candidates. However, in Sweden, the electorate is provided with the option of voting for the party list or for an individual candidate from the list, referred to as a personalized vote. For an individual candidate to be elected over the party list (i.e., for an individual to be awarded a seat before a party ranked candidate) they must receive enough individual votes to equal at least "8% of the party vote in the constituency."[52] Any candidate on the list that meets or exceeds this threshold would be ranked according to the number of votes they received, and seats would be allocated based on this ranking. If no candidate reaches the threshold, or if there are more seats than candidates meeting the threshold, then seats are allocated based on the party's list ranking. Although Sweden uses a list-PR system, how they determine the weight given to an individual candidate (personalized vote) could be useful for developing a flexible list in the Canadian context. Using British Columbia as an example, table 13 illustrates how a threshold could work within the Commission's proposed mixed member proportional system.

This is not the only method for determining the allocation of seats within a "flexible" list system.[53] However, regardless of the method chosen, the goal should be to balance the voter choice commonly associated with open lists with the goal of promoting women, minority group members and Aboriginal people.

Table 13 Awarding seats in a flexible list system
Red Party provincial–territorial votes in British Columbia

Red Party	Red Party
Party/Provincial-Territorial Vote	Party/Provincial-Territorial Vote
This is the total number of votes the Red Party received on the provincial/territorial portion of the ballot. Voters who selected the party chose to not indicate a preference for an individual candidate. The ranking established by the party (as appears in column under "Candidate Name") would therefore be used to allocate seats.	This is the list ranked by the party, and the number of voters who chose to indicate a preference for an individual candidate is illustrated in the column "Total Individual Votes." A vote for an individual candidate is a vote for this person to be allocated a party list seat. In order for an individual candidate to be selected over the party list ranking, they must receive enough votes to equal 8% or more of the Total Party Vote (50,000 in this example).

Party Name	Total Party Votes	Candidate Name	Total Individual Votes (% of Party Vote)
❑ Red Party	50,000	❑ 1. Candidate A	800 (1.6%)
		❑ 2. Candidate B	500 (1%)
		❑ 3. Candidate C	1,500 (3%)
		❑ 4. Candidate D	1,400 (2.8%)
		❑ 5. Candidate E	5,000 (10%)
		❑ 6. Candidate F	1,000 (2%)
		❑ 7. Candidate G	4,000 (8%)
		❑ 8. Candidate H	0 (0%)
		❑ 9. Candidate I	900 (1.8%)
		❑ 10. Candidate J	0 (0%)

Within the context of our proposed mixed member proportional system, suppose it is determined that the Red party should receive four list seats in British Columbia. In this case, we would need to determine which Red party members would fill those seats, i.e., whether the compensation seats would go to the candidates on the list established by the party or to an individual candidate on the list. To do this we would look at the total number of party votes that the Red party received on the provincial/territorial portion of the vote, which in this example is 50,000 votes (total party vote results are illustrated in the column, "Total Party Votes").

The next step in allocating the Red Party list seats would be to determine whether any individual candidate received enough votes to be entitled to a list seat before a candidate from the party ranked list. In other words, did any of the candidates receive enough individual votes to equal or exceed 8 percent of the "Total Party Votes"? We can see by looking at table 13 under "Total Individual Votes" that two candidates met or exceeded the established threshold. Candidate E received 5,000 Individual Votes, which is 10 percent of the Total Party Votes, and Candidate G received 4,000 Individual Votes, which is 8 percent of the Total Party Votes. In this instance, we would then rank order candidates E and G according to the number votes received and award the first two seats to these candidates, despite the fact the party had ranked these candidates 5th and 7th, respectively.

The final step would be to allocate the remaining two Red Party list seats. In this instance, candidates E and G would be removed from the list since they received the first two Red Party list seats. The remaining candidates on the list would then be re-ordered, and the two remaining list seats would be allocated to the top two candidates. In this instance, the top two candidates—A and B—retain their party ranking, and would be awarded the final two list seats for the Red Party.

We believe that a flexible list system represents a reasonable compromise for the Canadian context. Elections Canada or other government body should therefore develop a methodology for determining which candidate or candidates should be awarded each list seat. Implementing a flexible list would send a signal to voters about their primacy in the process of determining who gets elected. It would also support voters who decide to trust a political party's choice of list candidates by allowing them to vote for the party slate. Therefore:

Recommendation 5

Within the context of a mixed member proportional system, Parliament should adopt a *flexible* list system that provides voters with the option of either endorsing the party "slate" or "ticket," or of indicating a preference for a candidate within the list.

4.5.2 Women's Representation

The potential of the open portion of a flexible list to contribute to the under-representation of women in the legislature is a serious concern when designing a voting system for Canada. Increased representation of women is an important reason for reforming Canada's first-past-the-post voting system. Women represent one-half of the Canadian population, but only one-fifth of the current Members of Parliament. As the Royal Commission on Electoral Reform and Party Financing (Lortie Commission) suggested more than a decade ago, this is unacceptable, and steps must be taken to promote the equal representation of women in the House of Commons.[54] As the Lortie Commission argued: "The representation of women shows not only a significant deficit, but also that this deficit has persisted over the seven decades since they first received the franchise. Furthermore, their under-representation cuts across all other segments of society. Among ethno-cultural groups, only 6 of 121 (5 percent) ethno-cultural MPs elected since 1965 were women. In 1988, only 2 of 48 women candidates from ethno-cultural groups were elected ... this serious under-representation of a significant portion of society has important implications. The legitimacy of our democratic institutions suffers as a consequence. As well, there is a legitimate public interest in having equitable representation so that public policy is sensitive to the concerns and interests of various segments of society."[55]

The introduction of some element of proportional representation will help to increase the number of women in the House of Commons. As some observers have noted, "[i]n proportional systems, women and minority candidates are seen as assets and are placed on parties' lists in an attempt to attract women and minority voters. It is important to be seen to be fair to women and minorities, especially when a party is presenting a national or regional list with many names on it."[56] In 1999, for example, the newly elected Scottish Parliament included 37 percent women, while in 2003 the Welsh assembly became the "first legislative body with equal numbers of men and women."[57] At the same time, however, reforming the electoral system to include an element of proportionality is not sufficient to ensure women's equal representation. "Political parties, even under PR [proportional representation], have to be committed to recruiting women candidates, to placing these candidates high on the party-list and, once elected to giving these Members of Parliament access to cabinet posts."[58] There are other issues that need further examination to promote women's equal representation in the legislature.

Within the context of the existing electoral system, the Lortie Commission identified several steps that should be taken to "enhance the representational profile of the House of Commons." For example, they suggested that party nomination and recruitment processes be reformed to remove barriers for women to enter the House of Commons.[59] They also recommended implementing incentives for parties to increase the proportion of women in the House of Commons: "any party with at least 20 per cent of its House of Commons caucus consisting of women MPs [Members of Parliament] would be eligible for a higher rate of election reimbursement."[60] They argued this incentive should be used until women represented at least 40 percent of the House Commons, or until after three general elections, when a review process should be undertaken to determine whether this measure should be "retained or adjusted."[61] Initiatives such as these should be explored within the context of a mixed member proportional system.

There are also examples from several countries that have introduced measures to promote women's representation, including initiatives by jurisdictions with proportional representation. For example, political parties in Sweden have adopted a quota system to ensure that at least 50 percent of the candidates on the party list are women. The Swedish Social Democratic Labour Party's list alternates between women and men. Women occupy 45 percent of the seats in the lower house in Sweden.[62]

Other initiatives have been developed in countries such as Pakistan, Afghanistan, South Africa, and France. Pakistan has a quota system requiring that one-third of the legislative seats at the sub-national level be reserved for women. Article 83 of Afghanistan's Constitution requires the "general and just representation of all people of the country," including a requirement that at least 25 percent of the seats be reserved for women. The South African *Municipal Structures Act* (1988) encourages parties to ensure that at least 50 percent of list candidates for local elections are women, although there is no penalty for parties that do not adhere to this law. Finally, in 2000, France introduced parity legislation that required parties to run equal numbers of men and women candidates. Fines are levied against parties that do not.[63] Although these initiatives

---

"In Canada, representation is also affected by a number of factors and issues, such as federalism (the division of power among levels of government and minority protection), bicameralism (Senate reform and enhancing the role of backbench MPs), the executive (the concentration of power in the hands of the Prime Minister and his inner circle), regionalism and multiculturalism (Canada is made up of many diverse and sometimes contradictory elements that representation cannot always reconcile). An overall reform of Canada's model of representation must take into account these other rules of the game in Canadian political society." [Translation]

M. Tremblay, *La Représentation Politique au Canada : sur quelques considérations théoriques et empiriques* (Ottawa: Law Commission of Canada, 2003).

have yet to fully produce the intended effect—for example, many parties in France have paid a fine for not instituting quotas—it illustrates a growing interest in exploring ways to promote women's equal participation in the political system. These efforts underscore the fact that Canada must seek measures, including and beyond adopting a mixed member proportional system, so that women are equally represented in the House of Commons.

At a recent Commission co-sponsored consultation event on women's representation in the House of Commons, participants discussed issues relating to women's representation, including women's nomination and election campaigns, quotas for ensuring adequate representation of women candidates, incentives for women to participate in politics, and the unique experiences of visible minority women candidates.[64] Changing the electoral system to include an element of proportionality becomes a necessary, but insufficient, reform for increasing women's political representation.

Considering the under-representation of women in the House of Commons, and given the initiatives that have been tried in many other countries around the world, Canada must explore strategies such as voluntary or legislatively imposed quotas, and financial incentives as recommended by the Lortie Commission, at least as a temporary measure until there is a critical mass of women in politics that can act as role models for future generations of women. The Commission believes it is necessary to promote women's equal representation in the House of Commons, which includes ongoing, transparent and accountable monitoring of the measures adopted to achieve this goal.

Recommendation 6

Parliament should require political parties to develop initiatives and policies to promote equal representation of women in the House of Commons. Parties should be instructed to consider a range of issues, including:

- **parity on party lists,**

- **the use of quotas for party lists and constituency nominations,**

- recruiting policies for women candidates,

- incentive measures for women to participate in politics,

- support for campaign financing, including measures to enhance access to candidacy, and

- the inclusion of more women in cabinet, if a party is elected as the government.

Following the first general election under the new electoral system, political parties should also be required to submit reports to Parliament outlining how they addressed these issues.

Recommendation 7

A Parliamentary committee should subsequently review the parties' reports on the measures they have taken to promote the equal representation of women in the House of Commons.

"What happens to the equality concern in the politics of cabinet coalitions? ... The answer is simple. The equality concern will become a non-concern. It will be completely forgotten. The political actors involved in putting together a coalition cabinet will possess varying agendas. Members of the largest party will seek a pre-eminence benefiting their numbers, a suitable measure of policy agreement with their new partners and the capacity to govern. Members of other minor parties will seek publicly prominent cabinet positions and possibly some policy commitments to the largest party. None will give a second's thought to the extent to which a coalition government or cabinet overall does or does not match the voting profile of the electorate ..."

P. Aucoin and J. Smith, "Proportional Representation: Misrepresenting Equality." *Policy Options* (1997) at 31.

4.5.3 Minority Group Representation

The inclusion of minority group candidates in our system of democratic governance is a closely related issue. As noted in Chapter 2 (see section 2.4.1), minority group candidates are under-represented in the House of Commons. The Royal Commission on Electoral Reform and Party Financing (Lortie Commission) suggested that ethno-cultural groups have experienced greater representation in the House of Commons, but that "visible minorities" were under-represented.[65] As with women's representation, there is a possibility that this will change with the introduction of a mixed member proportional system. And, similarly, simply adding an element of proportional representation is not sufficient. Minority group candidates face many of the same issues and challenges as women do. Party lists, access to cabinet positions once elected, incentives for visible minority candidates, and campaign financing, among other issues, are important concerns. The Commission believes it is necessary to promote the greater representation of minority group candidates in the House of Commons, which includes ongoing, transparent and accountable monitoring of the measures adopted to achieve this goal.

Recommendation 8

Parliament should require political parties to develop initiatives and policies to promote greater representation of minority group members in the House of Commons. Parties should be instructed to consider a range of issues, including:

- **minority group candidates on party lists,**
- **the use of quotas for party lists and constituency nominations,**
- **recruiting policies for minority group candidates,**
- **incentive measures for minority group candidates to participate in politics,**
- **support for campaign financing, including measures to enhance access to candidacy, and**

- the inclusion of more minority group members in cabinet, if a party is elected as the government.

Following the first general election under the new electoral system, political parties should also be required to submit reports to Parliament outlining how they addressed these issues.

Recommendation 9

A Parliamentary committee should subsequently review the parties' reports on the measures they have taken to promote greater representation of minority group members in the House of Commons.

> "There are many issues we could explore to increase our understanding of ethnocultural and visible minority groups and their political participation in Canada. One of the most important is how to increase the representation of groups traditionally left out of the electoral and decision-making processes. In essence, that is also a pathway to encouraging representative democracy."
>
> C. Simard, "Political Participation by Ethnocultural Groups and Visible Minorities" 5:2 *Horizons* 2002 at 11.

4.5.4 Youth Representation

Another issue that needs to be addressed is the participation of youth in our system of democratic governance. While a mixed member proportional system has the potential to foster a greater diversity and plurality of voices, this benefit will not necessarily address the unique issues of youth participation and representation in our political processes.

As noted in Chapter 2 (section 2.4.4), there are many factors that contribute to youths' lack of participation in the electoral system, such as insufficient political knowledge, lack of time to vote, feeling disconnected from the system of democratic governance, and disinterest in politics.[66] Concern over youth participation recently led the Chief Electoral Officer of Canada, Jean Pierre Kingsley, to undertake a major initiative to address the declining voter turnout among youth.[67] As part of this initiative, in October 2003, Elections Canada hosted a National Forum on Youth Voting to explore the reasons behind declining youth electoral participation, provide youth with the opportunity to share their thoughts on how to improve youth voter turnout, and develop measures to "encourage youth electoral participation."[68]

Young people face challenges similar to those facing women and members of minority groups. Canadian youth are marginalized from the system of democratic governance. They desire a more meaningful voice in the system of governance, and express concern about issues such as low youth voter turnout, political education, and the disinterest evidenced by many politicians in youth issues. We need to explore ideas for soliciting youths' ideas, whether it is through introducing measures to give them a voice in government decision making, or by modernizing the processes for participating in the electoral system (e.g., introducing Internet voter registration and voting). To develop the next generation of voters, the current electoral system should be adapted to the needs of young people and to the ideas and issues that they find important.

The issue of youth representation and participation not only raises fundamental questions about the inclusion of younger people in our democracy, but more generally about the way in which youth are treated in our society. If Parliament and provincial legislatures are to more accurately reflect the diverse society in which we live, then including a youth voice in government decision-making processes becomes an important aspect of any reform agenda.

Recommendation 10

Parliament should require that political parties examine options for increasing youth participation and representation in mainstream political decision making. This process should be based on broad and inclusive consultations, and should consider ways to better reflect the perspectives of youth in the system of democratic governance. Political parties should also be required to submit reports to Parliament outlining the measures they have taken to promote youth participation and representation. A Parliamentary committee should subsequently review the parties' reports.

4.6 Aboriginal People's Representation in the New Electoral System[69]

Electoral system designers must also take into consideration the importance of demographic representation when they create a Canadian version of a mixed member proportional system. They must particularly address the question of whether to incorporate separate seats for First Nations, Inuit, and Métis peoples, as New Zealand does for the Maori; create an Aboriginal regional list or multi-member constituency that would perhaps overlap several provinces; or introduce a separate Aboriginal Parliament. It must be established at the outset that the adoption of any of these options should not derogate from the right to self-government or any other Aboriginal ancestral right. Two examples from other jurisdictions provide useful and relevant information—the experiences of New Zealand and the state of Maine in the United States.

4.6.1 New Zealand

The Maori are the indigenous people of New Zealand, comprising roughly 10 percent of the country's population. Their early relationship with the pākehā, or white settlers, was very turbulent and eventually culminated in the "New Zealand Wars" (1843–1872).[70] The fact that the Maori were still a powerful group even after their defeat by the settlers had an impact on their treatment by the New Zealand government. The passage of the *Maori Representation Act* in 1867 provided the Maori with four guaranteed seats in the House of Representatives.[71]

Although the original system for electing Maori representatives was complex and problematic, it was retained almost unchanged for more than 125 years. After New Zealand's binding referendum on electoral reform, the government revised the Maori electoral system in the 1993 *Electoral Act.* As before, Maori voters were required to choose whether to be listed on the Maori electoral rolls or on the general rolls. However, where the number of Maori seats had previously been frozen at four, the new legislation provided that the number of Maori seats would be increased to proportionally represent the number of electors on the Maori rolls. It also reduced the number of general seats from 95 to 60, again based on proportionality. Following the 2002 General Election, there are seven Maori seats in New Zealand's House of Representatives.[72] Maori candidates can also be elected to general seats.

There is some debate as to whether this method of representation is effective. Some observers argue that Maori representation under New Zealand's mixed member proportional system is fair in the sense that the number of Maori Members of Parliament is proportionate to the number of Maori in the general population. However, they also argue that in terms of "effective representation," which refers to the ability of a group to advance its interests, the New Zealand system still needs improvement.[73]

4.6.2　Maine

The state of Maine also uses a system of guaranteed representation for its Aboriginal population, which is comprised of the Penobscot and Passamaquoddy tribes. This began informally as early as 1823, when the Penobscot people sent their first recorded representative to the State Legislature. The arrangement was formalized in 1866 for the Penobscot tribe and in 1927 for the Passamaquoddy.[74] Each tribe was granted a single representative in the State Legislature.

Aboriginal electors are entitled to vote for *both* an Aboriginal candidate and also for a candidate on the general electoral ballot. Because of this duality, Members of the State Legislature (MSLs) who are elected to the guaranteed Aboriginal seats do not have the full range of powers that candidates elected on the general ballot possess. Specifically, guaranteed-seat MSLs are not permitted to vote on or introduce legislation into the state legislature. However, they have all the other powers and privileges that regular MSLs possess.[75] There are no provisions in Maine's electoral law that allow for an increase or decrease in the number of guaranteed seats. This is not a live issue at present, however, as the state's Aboriginal population—approximately 4500—is not that large.[76]

4.6.3 Royal Commission on Electoral Reform and Party Financing

In Canada, the Royal Commission on Electoral Reform and Party Financing (Lortie Commission) studied the question of Aboriginal electoral districts.[77] The report suggests that Canada ought to learn from the New Zealand model and create its own version of Aboriginal representation in Parliament. During their consultations, the Lortie Commission learned that there was broad support among Aboriginal people for Aboriginal seats.[78]

The principal recommendations of the Lortie Commission for the creation of Aboriginal Electoral Districts (AEDs) were as follows.[79]

- "Aboriginal Voters would have the choice of registering as Aboriginal voters or on the general voters lists in the regular constituency in which they reside … This choice would have to be made, however, before the boundaries of the constituencies were drawn. … Once this decision on registration was made, any Aboriginal voter who wished to switch from one list to the other could not do so until the time of the next election …"[80]

- "Aboriginal seats would be created only when the number of people registered as Aboriginal voters in a province met the minimum number required for a constituency in accordance with the principle of representation by population. In this way, Aboriginal constituencies would satisfy the general criterion of equality of the vote."[81]

- The AEDs would be contained within provincial boundaries, although they might overlap existing constituencies geographically.

- Where the number of voters on the Aboriginal register warranted the creation of more than one constituency in any given province, the relevant electoral boundaries commission could "create two or more Aboriginal constituencies on a geographical basis or on the basis of distinct Aboriginal peoples within the province. *In either case, the commission would make its decisions following discussions and public hearings involving Aboriginal people.*"[82]

- That "the number of Aboriginal constituencies in a province should be equal to such integer as is obtained by dividing the number of voters on the Aboriginal voters register by a number equal to 85 per cent of the electoral quotient for the province."[83]

- The Aboriginal populations in each of the Atlantic provinces would not (as of 1991—and the same is true in 2003) justify the creation of an AED in any of them, but the *combined Aboriginal populations* in the region would warrant the creation of a single AED for the entire area. "The creation of an Aboriginal constituency for Atlantic Canada, cutting across provincial boundaries, would ... require a constitutional amendment by Parliament analogous to its creation of seats in the two federal territories. Given that Atlantic Canada is already over-represented as a region, we support the Committee for Aboriginal Electoral Reform proposal that the *federal and provincial governments* concerned meet with Aboriginal leaders in the area to determine how a seat could be allocated through a constitutional amendment ..."[84]

Using the formula established by the Lortie Commission (one AED for every quotient equal to 85 percent of the provincial electoral quotient) and 2001 census data for Aboriginal populations by province, we can estimate that eight or perhaps nine Aboriginal constituencies would be created, depending on the proportion of Aboriginal voters who placed themselves on the Aboriginal list.[85] This formula is restrictive and does raise questions of equity, however: the approximately 54,000 Aboriginals living in the Atlantic provinces would be deprived of a representative; and neither would Quebec's 80,000 Aboriginals warrant the creation of an AED in that province.[86]

4.6.4 Royal Commission on Aboriginal Peoples

The Royal Commission on Aboriginal Peoples advocated the creation of a separate Aboriginal Parliament in its 1996 report: "we are concerned that efforts to reform the Senate and the House of Commons may not be compatible with the foundations for a renewed relationship built upon the inherent right of Aboriginal self-government and nation-to-nation governmental relations. Three orders of government imply the existence of representative institutions that provide for some degree of majority control, *not minority or supplementary status.*"[87]

According to the Royal Commission on Aboriginal Peoples (RCAP), an Aboriginal Parliament, or "House of First Peoples," should initially act as an advisory body. It would provide advice on anything that affects Aboriginal interests, directly or indirectly, and could receive references from the House of Commons or Senate for investigations.[88] In addition, however, the Royal Commission on Aboriginal Peoples argued that to have a real impact, the House of First Peoples would eventually need "real power." This was defined as "the power to initiate legislation and to require a majority vote on matters critical to the lives of Aboriginal peoples."[89] Because the addition of a third legislative body with such powers would require a constitutional amendment, the Royal Commission on Aboriginal Peoples recommended that the House of First Peoples initially be created by Parliament, in consultation with Aboriginal groups, as an advisory body only.

According to the Royal Commission on Aboriginal Peoples, Aboriginal peoples should elect members to the Aboriginal Parliament. They recommend at least one member of the Aboriginal Parliament for each Aboriginal nation. They further suggest that larger groups like the Cree or Ojibwa First Nations might be entitled to more than one member. Enumeration of Aboriginal voters would take place at the same time as enumeration for federal elections. Likewise, elections for the House of First Peoples would take place at the same time as federal elections, in order to add legitimacy to the process.[90]

Both the Royal Commission on Electoral Reform and Party Financing and the Royal Commission on Aboriginal Peoples raise fundamental questions regarding the representation of First Nation, Métis, and Inuit people in the House of Commons. Although they put forth different recommendations, they both underscore the importance of developing methods for increasing the voice of Aboriginal peoples in the system of democratic governance. Our proposal to award list seats in the territories will partly increase the number of Aboriginal people in the House of Commons. At the same time, however, we also believe that additional strategies must be developed in consultation with First Nations, Métis and Inuit peoples to ensure better representation of these groups in Parliament.

Recommendation 11

Parliament should require political parties, in consultation with First Nations, Métis and Inuit peoples, to develop initiatives and policies to promote greater representation of Aboriginal people in the House of Commons. Parties should be instructed to consider a range of issues, including:

- **Aboriginal candidates on party lists,**

- **the use of quotas for party lists and constituency nominations,**

- **recruiting policies for Aboriginal candidates,**

- **incentive measures for Aboriginal peoples to participate in politics,**

- **support for campaign financing, including measures to enhance access to candidacy, and**

- **the inclusion of Aboriginal people in cabinet, if a party is elected as the government.**

Following the first general election under the new electoral system, political parties should also be required to submit reports to Parliament outlining how they addressed these issues. A Parliamentary committee should subsequently review the parties' reports on the measures they have taken to promote greater representation of Aboriginal people in the House of Commons.

Recommendation 12

The federal government, in consultation with First Nations, Métis, and Inuit peoples, should explore the possibility of introducing Aboriginal Electoral Districts, as recommended

by the Royal Commission on Electoral Reform and Party Financing, or a "House of Aboriginal Peoples", consistent with the recommendations of the Royal Commission on Aboriginal Peoples.

"There has been a general feeling among Aboriginal people that the electoral system is so stacked against them that AEDs are the only way they can gain representation in parliament in proportion to their numbers. Direct representation of Aboriginal people would help to overcome long-standing concerns that the electoral process has not accommodated the Aboriginal community of interest and identity. Aboriginal [voters] would elect Members of Parliament who would represent them and be directly accountable to them at regular intervals. MPs from [Aboriginal constituencies] would understand their Aboriginal constituents, their rights, interests and perspectives on the full range of national public policy issues."

Committee for Aboriginal Electoral Reform, cited in Canada,
Royal Commission on Electoral Reform and Party Financing,
Final Report: Reforming Electoral Democracy
(Ottawa: Minister of Supply and Services, 1991) Vol. IV at 274.

4.7 Electoral System Design Issues

4.7.1 Including Diverse Voices: Thresholds

One of the questions that must be addressed when designing a mixed member proportional system for Canada is whether or not to establish a legal threshold for access to the list seats. This raises important questions because it relates directly to the criteria of encouraging a diversity or plurality of voices in legislatures. In Germany, a party must win either three direct mandates (constituency seats) or 5 percent of the *nation-wide* vote to qualify for list seats. This is a quite formidable barrier to break through—intentionally so, to discourage extremist parties from gaining representation in the *Bundestag*. In New Zealand, the threshold is 5 percent of the national vote or one direct mandate.

We also need to consider instances when a party does not contest any constituency seats, but instead chooses to focus their electoral campaigns on the provincial or territorial compensation seats (e.g., they could rely on the fact that they would still be considered for a compensatory seat despite the fact they did not contest and therefore did not win a single constituency seat). This situation may not be fair to other parties that have to balance their time and resources working on both constituency and provincial or territorial list campaigns. It is indeed critical that the electoral rules not undermine the importance of the constituency vote for the system to work appropriately. The Jenkins Commission recommended that a party be eligible for compensatory list seats only if it presents candidates in at least 50 percent of the ridings in the regional district.[91] The Law Commission believes that a requirement of at least one-third would minimize the risk of having a large number of very marginal parties being voted into Parliament. This threshold would not prevent parties from running and participating in electoral campaigns,[92] but would prevent a possible distortion of the system and its balance between constituency and list votes.

In addition, the de facto thresholds established by the magnitude of the compensatory districts in the proposed model would likely prevent a large number of marginal parties from being voted in without having to secure a large support base in the voting population, while maintaining the goal of encouraging a diversity of people and ideas (e.g., new and different political parties) in the system of democratic governance. At the same time, it does not prevent the introduction of new voices into the House of Commons or a provincial legislature.

Recommendation 13

There should be no legal threshold for gaining access to the list (compensatory) seats.

Recommendation 14

A party should be eligible for compensatory provincial list seats only if it presents candidates for election in at least one-third of the constituencies in the relevant province. In Prince Edward Island, any party wishing to be eligible for the list seats would have to contest the single-member constituency seat in that province. In Nunavut, Northwest Territories, and Yukon, any party wishing to be eligible for a list seat would have to contest the single-member constituency seat in the relevant territory.

4.7.2   Accountability: Double Inclusion

Another question to be addressed is whether restrictions ought to be placed on candidates seeking to run at both the constituency level and on the provincial or regional party list. Typically, party elites favour this form of *double inclusion,* since it maximizes the chances for election of "star" candidates: if they fail to win in the constituency race, they can hedge their bets by securing a high ranking on the party's regional or provincial list. Some observers have criticized this favourable treatment of candidates who fail to win a constituency seat, arguing that it allows second-rank candidates to gain entry to the legislature through the back door. However, a number of countries—Italy, for example—actually allot compensatory seats to the "best losers" in the constituency races. Research shows that "only Thailand has ever banned double inclusion, and Mexico is the only other system to have imposed any legal limits on it."[93] The flexible party list as proposed in this Report ought to minimize any potential voter unhappiness with some candidates trying to maximize their chances for election by running at both levels.[94]

Recommendation 15

There should be no legal restrictions on *double inclusion.* That is, candidates should be able to run both in a constituency and on the party list at the provincial or territorial level.

4.8 Conclusion

This Report's survey of the various electoral options for Canada has led to the conclusion that adding an element of proportionality to Canada's electoral system, as inspired by the systems currently used in Scotland and Wales, would be the most appropriate model for adoption. This system would even out the regional imbalances in party caucuses produced by our first-past-the-post system. It would produce highly proportional results, as the data in table 11 indicate. This model would have additional implications, which will be discussed in Chapter 5.

---

1 A. Reynolds and B. Reilly, *The International IDEA Handbook of Electoral System Design*, 2nd ed. (Stockholm: International Institute for Democracy and Electoral Assistance, 1997) at 44.

2 See, for example, D.M. Farrell, *Comparing Electoral Systems* (London: Prentice Hall, 1997) at Table 7.1.

3 Electoral Reform Society, "French Presidential Election 2002: Failings of the Second Ballot System" (London, April 2002) at 4.

4 Reynolds and Reilly, *supra* note 1 at 38.

5 B. Schwartz and D. Rettie, "Valuing Canadians: The Options for Voting System Reform in Canada" (Ottawa: Law Commission of Canada, 2002) at 57.

6 Schwartz and Rettie quote Winston Churchill's verdict on the alternative vote: it is "the worst of all possible plans ... the stupidest, the least scientific and the most unreal. The decision ... is to be determined by the most worthless votes given to the most worthless candidates." Schwartz and Rettie, *ibid.*

7 Farrell, *supra* note 2 at 110–11.

8 Farrell, *supra* note 2 at Table 7.1.

9 J. A. Cousins, *Electoral Reform for Prince Edward Island: A Discussion Paper* (Charlottetown: Institute of Island Studies at the University of Prince Edward Island, 2000) at 24. Farrell notes that New York state briefly adopted the single transferable vote for municipal elections in the 1930s. "In one case, in

Brooklyn, the constituency was so large that 99 candidates put their names forward for election. The ballot paper was more than four feet long!" Farrell, *supra* note 2 at 128.

10 United Kingdom, Independent Commission on the Voting System [Jenkins Commission] *Final Report*, 1998 at para. 95.

11 Cousins, *supra* note 9 at 24.

12 Farrell, *supra* note 2 at 123.

13 According to Brams and Fishburn, a "preferential voting system is monotonic if more first-place votes can never hurt a candidate." For a discussion of this supposed "logical flaw" in single transferable vote and alternative vote, see Farrell, *supra* note 2 at 135–36. Mathematicians and political scientists have noted that it is theoretically possible for a candidate's chances for election to be *reduced* as he or she receives more first-place votes. The technical literature refers to this as a "non-monotonic" outcome. Some observers argue that this feature of single transferable vote (and other preferential voting systems such as alternative vote) "violates … a fundamental democratic ethic, others point out that it rarely occurs in practice." See, J. Brams and P.C. Fishburn, "Some Logical Defects of the Single Transferable Vote" in A. Lijphart and B. Grofman eds., *Choosing an Electoral System: Issues and Alternatives* (New York: Praeger, 1984) at 151 and 152.

14 Reynolds and Reilly, *supra* note 1 at 65.

15 *Panachage* is the most "open" form of ballot structure available in certain countries using list-PR (Luxembourg and Switzerland, notably). Voters may give preferences to candidates from more than one party (Farrell, *supra* note 2 at 173). This is also called a free list. Reynolds and Reilly, *ibid.* at 60.

16 Farrell, *supra* note 2 at 167; M.S. Shugart and M.P. Wattenberg, "Conclusion: Are Mixed-Member Systems the Best of Both Worlds?" in M.S. Shugart and M.P. Wattenberg, eds., *Mixed-Member Electoral Systems: The Best of Both Worlds?* (Oxford: Oxford University Press, 2001) at 571–96.

17 Hungary, for instance, employs a two-round system to elect representatives in the single-member constituencies. The Jenkins Commission in the United Kingdom recommended that the alternative vote be used in the plurality component of a new electoral system. For an exhaustive survey of the numerous types of mixed system currently employed in the world, see L. Massicotte and A. Blais, "Mixed Electoral Systems: A Conceptual and Empirical Survey" (1998) 18:3 *Electoral Studies* at 341.

18 H. Milner, "The Case for Proportional Representation" (1997) *Policy Options* 18:9 at 7.

19 In Scotland and Wales, the European Parliament constituencies, created in 1994, are used as the regional districts, while in Germany the Lander (states) are the basis for assigning the compensatory seats. In Germany, "[e]ach voter has 2 votes: 1 ('first vote') for an individual candidate in one of the constituencies, and 1 ('second vote') for the party-list established, for each of the Land, by each political party. Half of the Deputies are elected from among the individual candidates and half of them on the basis of the lists. Among candidates from a given constituency, the candidate having received the highest number of first votes becomes Deputy." Inter-Parliamentary Union, <http://www.ipu.org> Information on Germany from <http://www.ipu.org/parline-e/reports/2121_B.htm> (date accessed: 19 December 2003). In each Land, every party is entitled to the number of seats that corresponds to its share in the second votes

20 The sparsely populated northern territories could either be folded into British Columbia and the prairies or be left out of the regional list voting altogether. Each of these regions would have a minimum of 12 compensatory seats, up to a maximum of 34 in Ontario. The advantage of using these larger districts for list seats is that they provide more proportional results than smaller districts, and make it easier for smaller parties to win representation in Parliament.

21 *Constitution Act*, 1867, (U.K.), 30 & 31 Vict., c. 3, s. 51A, reprinted in R.S.C. 1985, App. II, No. 5.

22 Canada, Task Force on Canadian Unity, *A Future Together: Observations and Recommendations* (Canada: Minister of Supply and Services, 1979) at 105.

23 A simulation of the 1980 election using that proposal demonstrated that the Liberal Party, with just over 44 percent of the popular vote, would have taken 27 (45 percent) of the list seats. These top-up seats would have been apportioned to provinces where the Liberal Party was under-represented (most notably Ontario, Alberta, and British Columbia). See, W. Irvine, *Does Canada Need a New Electoral System?* (Kingston: Institute of Intergovernmental Relations, Queen's University, 1979) at 86–90.

24 Canada, *supra* note 22 at 106. A similar proposal, put forth by one electoral system observer, includes the addition of 29 top-up seats to the 301 constituency seats in the House of Commons, distributed among the provinces according to population. As with the Task Force proposal, in this model the party that benefits the most from first-past-the-post (the Liberals) would also have received the largest share of compensation seats if the mixed system had been

used for the 1997 federal election. The Liberals would have been awarded 11 of the top-up seats, the Reform Party 11, the Progressive Conservative Party 6, and the New Democratic Party 1. The Liberals would have ended up with 166 seats in the 330-seat House of Commons. In other words, the Liberals' 38 percent of the vote in 1997 would have translated into 50.3 percent of the seats (as opposed to the 51.5 percent they obtained under first-past-the-post). See, K. Weaver, "MMP is Too Much of Some Good Things" in H. Milner ed., *Making Every Vote Count: Reassessing Canada's Electoral System* (Peterborough: Broadview Press, 1999) at table 5-1.

25   The calculation is as follows: 172 x .67 = 115.24. Because of the distribution of seats in each province, this is rounded up to 116.

26   The list seats would be assigned on the basis of the d'Hondt method, although in principle any of the various formulas (Hare, Droop, Imperiali, Saint-Laguë, etc.) for awarding list seats could be employed. Lijphart states that the d'Hondt method is the most frequently used proportional representation formula in the established democracies. It is a *highest average formula*, as opposed to a largest remainder formula such as the Hare and Imperiali quotas. Each of these different methods has a specific impact on overall proportionality; some, like the Imperiali and d'Hondt formulas, favour the large parties, while others (Saint-Laguë) are more beneficial to smaller parties. A. Lijphart, *Electoral Systems and Party Systems: A Study of Twenty-Seven Democracies, 1945-1990* (Oxford: Oxford University Press, 1994) at 21. For an example of a calculation based on d'Hondt divisors, see the Quebec Green Paper (Québec, Ministre d'État à la Réforme électorale et parlementaire, *One Citizen, One Vote: Green Paper on the Reform of the Electoral System*. Éditeur official du Québec, 1979).

27   M.S. Shugart and M.P. Wattenberg, "Mixed-Member Systems: A Definition and Typology" in M.S. Shugart and M.P. Wattenberg, eds., *Mixed-Member Electoral Systems: The Best of Both Worlds?* (Oxford: Oxford University Press, 2001) at 16. (Emphasis added.)

28   Proportionality depends to a very large extent on the existence of thresholds (that is, whether or not a party needs to attain a certain percentage of the popular vote in order to be awarded list seats) and district magnitude in the proportional representation tier.

29   Even if, in Germany, the ballot informs voters that the vote for a constituency representative is the "primary vote" (*Erststimme*). According to Farrell, this is a psychological nuance "intended to create the impression that the constituency vote is more significant," even though the reverse is true. Farrell, *supra* note 2 at 91.

30 Scotland is divided into eight parliamentary regions, each with seven list seats.

31 Note that the share of list seats increases to 40 percent from 33 percent in the mixed member majoritarian and mixed member proportional (Scottish model) systems. This is done primarily to offset the skewed constituency results in Ontario, where the Liberals won 97 percent of the seats but only 52 percent of the vote. Had the split between first-past-the-post and proportional representation seats remained at two-thirds/one-third, as with the other two models, a total of *twelve* extra, or "overhang" seats would have been required to provide the other parties with their rightful share of the list seats. With a 60/40 split between first-past-the-post and proportional representation seats, only five overhang seats are required (we discuss this notion of overhang seats more fully below).

32 In the 1949 election in West Germany, the 5 percent threshold was set at the regional level (the *Länder*). This led to an increased number of parties gaining election to the Bundestag. See H-D. Klingemann and B. Wessels, "The Political Consequences of Germany's Mixed-Member System: Personalization at the Grass Roots?" in M.S. Shugart and M.P. Wattenberg, eds., *Mixed-Member Electoral Systems: The Best of Both Worlds?* (Oxford: Oxford University Press, 2001) at 282–85. One of the worries about provincial thresholds in Canada is that they would "be unlikely to exclude regionally focused parties." K. Weaver, "MMP is Too Much of Some Good Things" in H. Milner, ed., *Making Every Vote Count* (Peterborough: Broadview Press, 1999) at 81. We will address this criticism in Chapter 5.

33 Farrell, *supra* note 2 at 93.

34 In 2000, the Liberals won 97 percent of the seats in the province, which in our version of the mixed member proportional model would have been the equivalent of 60 seats. Their share of the provincial vote, however, was only 52 percent, which would entitle them to 55 seats.

35 Alternatively, one could adopt the approach that has been used in Bolivia since it established a mixed member proportional electoral system in 1994. In that country, if a party wins more than its rightful share of constituency seats in a given region, "the number of seats to be allocated to party lists in the district is reduced. Specifically, the law provides that the party or parties receiving the lowest share of seats shall be deprived of seats." R.A. Mayorga, "Electoral Reform in Bolivia: Origins of the Mixed-Member Proportional System" in M.S. Shugart and M.P. Wattenberg, eds., *Mixed-Member Electoral Systems: The Best of Both Worlds?* (Oxford: Oxford University Press 2001) at 203. Again, such a solution seems to run counter to the objectives of equity, fairness, and inclusiveness (facilitating the election of "new voices" represented by the smaller parties).

36 In Germany, the number of overhang seats was typically quite small in any given election, ranging from zero to five, at least until unification. Since 1990, however, the number of such seats has increased to the mid-teens. See H-D. Klingemann and B. Wessels, "The Political Consequences of Germany's Mixed-Member System: Personalization at the Grass Roots?" in M.S. Shugart and M.P. Wattenberg *Mixed-Member Electoral Systems: The Best of Both Worlds?* (Oxford: Oxford University Press, 2001) at 286.

37 *Constitution Act,* 1982, being Schedule B to the *Canada Act,* 1982 (U.K.), 1982, c.11. For example, if a party obtains an overwhelmingly disproportionate number of seats on the constituency (first-past-the-post) portion of the ballot, and also performs well on the regional (proportional representation) portion of the ballot, then the number of overhang seats (electoral bonus) that they obtain might result in that province having more seats in the House of Commons than is constitutionally permissible. To provide further context, suppose that a province constitutes 10 percent of the country's population, entitling it to 10 percent of the seats in the House of Commons (essentially 30 of the 301 seats). Based on the mixed member proportional system, two-thirds of the province's 30 seats (20 seats) would be decided based on first-past-the-post, the remaining one-third through proportional representation (10 seats). In this scenario, it is possible that a party could win a majority of the constituency seats (e.g., 15 seats) as well as perform well on the proportional representation portion of the ballot, entitling it to an additional 5 seats. At the same time, other parties that split the remaining 5 constituency seats could also be entitled to top-up seats based on their performance on the proportional representation side of the ballot (e.g., 8 additional seats). As a result, the province could be assigned a total of 33 seats, 20 constituency seats, plus 8 top-up seats: 3 more seats than is constitutionally permissible.

38 For a discussion of the constitutional implications of many past proposals for electoral reform in Canada, see W. Irvine, "A Review and Evaluation of Electoral System Reform Proposals" in P. Aucoin, ed., *Institutional Reforms for Representative Government.* Volume 38 of the Research Studies commissioned for the Royal Commission on the Economic Union and Development Prospects for Canada (Toronto: University of Toronto Press, 1985) at 103–106. In this particular case, because it is Ontario that would receive the additional overhang seats, there is not likely to be a constitutional problem, since the province is presently under-represented in the House of Commons. In 2000, Ontario's population of 11.2 million represented 38 percent of the total population in the country. Its 103 seats in the House of Commons, however, constitute 34.2 percent of the total seats, meaning that Ontario is under-represented by 3.8 percentage points. British Columbia is also under-represented (1.7 percent in

2000), while the Atlantic provinces as a whole (+3 percent) and Saskatchewan (+1.4 percent) are over-represented. These figures will change slightly with the next redistribution, which will award 3 additional seats to Ontario and 2 each to Alberta and British Columbia.

39 This is a variation of the d'Hondt divisor. The formula is: total regional votes/(constituencies won + 1). The addition of the one in the denominator ensures that even parties that did not win a seat in a given region will be eligible for the compensatory list seats. This yields a "regional figure," or divisor, and the party with the highest divisor is awarded the first regional seat. Each time a party wins a regional seat, the denominator is increased by 1 for that party, and the process is repeated until all of the regional seats are filled.

40 Based on our decision to assign list seats by province, in this example, Prince Edward Island has one single-seat constituency and three compensatory list seats; Newfoundland has four single-seat constituencies and three list seats, and so on. In the four Atlantic provinces, 60 percent of the total constituencies in the region are single-seat districts determined by the first-past-the-post electoral formula, and the remaining 40 percent are compensatory seats determined by the version of the d'Hondt formula employed in Scotland. In the rest of the country, the split between first-past-the-post constituencies and list seats is two-thirds/one-third. Because of the relatively smaller populations represented in most of the constituencies in the Atlantic provinces, we can afford to reduce the number of first-past-the-post ridings by a greater factors than in the rest of the country. This keeps the average population of constituencies in the different regions of the country more or less in line with one another. Because of the size of Quebec and Ontario, we have divided each into smaller regions. In Quebec, we have created two regions, essentially corresponding to Quebec outside of Montreal and Montreal itself. Each region has approximately the same population (3.6 million and 3.5 million) along with similar numbers of single-seat districts and regional compensatory seats (12 and 11). In Ontario, we have established three regions, corresponding roughly to north/east Ontario, Toronto region, and south/west Ontario. As with Quebec, each region has roughly the same population (between 3.5 and 3.6 million) and similar numbers of single-seat districts and compensatory seats (11 or 12 in the case of the latter). Detailed information on how the five regions were produced can be found in Appendix A.

41 R. Taagepera and M.S. Shugart, *Seats and Votes* (New Haven and London: Yale University Press, 1989) at 106, 131.

42 It would be possible to design this mixed member proportional system based on a ballot with a single option: voters would cast their votes strictly for a single

candidate in a traditional constituency, and these votes would then be aggregated according to any of a number of different formulas in order to award party list seats at the provincial level in order to compensate for distortions in the first-past-the-post results. William Irvine has devised just such a single-vote system that would have produced highly proportional election results. See W. Irvine, *supra* note 23 at 35.

43 United Kingdom, Independent Commission on the Electoral System, *Final Report* (1998) at para. 139.

44 F. Barker, J. Boston, S. Levine, E. McLeay, and N.S. Roberts, "An Initial Assessment of the Consequences of MMP in New Zealand" in M.S. Shugart and M.P. Wattenberg, eds., *Mixed Member Electoral Systems: The Best of Both Worlds?* (Oxford: Oxford University Press, 2001) at 310, quoting S. Levine and N.S. Roberts, "MMP: The Decision" in R. Miller, ed., *New Zealand Politics in Transition* (Auckland: Oxford University Press, 1997) at 186.

45 The number of candidates on the Party/Regional portion of the ballot in figure 4 is for illustrative purposes only. Based on our proposed Scottish model of two-thirds first-past-the-post and one-third proportional representation, there would be a maximum of 13 candidates on the regional/party list portion of the ballot.

46 J. Vowles, J. Karp and S. Banducci, "Proportional Representation on Trial: Elite vs. Mass Opinion on Electoral System Change in New Zealand." Paper prepared for the annual meeting of the American Political Science Association, Washington, DC (30 August–3 September 2000).

47 Farrell, *supra* note 2 at 76.

48 R. Katz, "Reforming the Italian Electoral Law, 1993" in M.S. Shugart and M.P. Wattenberg, eds., *Mixed Member Electoral Systems: The Best of Both Worlds?* (Oxford: Oxford University Press, 2001) at 97.

49 D. MacShane, "Open Lists Will give Us Closed Minds," *The New Statesman* (27 November 1998) at 127.

50 One study suggests that "the implementation of gender quotas in open-list proportional systems will not have as positive an effect on the percentage of women elected as has been the case in closed-list systems ... Nevertheless, these findings indicate that even in many open-list systems, quotas are likely to increase the percentage of women elected ..." M.P. Jones and P. Navia, "Assessing the Effectiveness of Gender Quotas in Open-List Proportional Representation Electoral Systems" (1999) 80:2 *Social Science Quarterly* at 353. Even though this

study was based on data from Latin American countries, there is reason to believe that the observations hold in the established democracies as well.

51 According to Shugart and Wattenberg, in flexible lists "there is a party-ordered list, but voters have the option of casting a preference vote. Voters who cast a party-list vote are assisting the election of candidates in the order they appear on the ballot … However … candidates who obtain an established quota of [preference] votes can move up ahead of copartisans whom the party ranked higher." M.S. Shugart and M.P. Wattenberg "Conclusion: Are Mixed-Member Systems the Best of Both Worlds?" in M.S. Shugart and M.P. Wattenberg, eds., *Mixed-Member Electoral Systems: The Best of Both Worlds?* (Oxford: Oxford University Press, 2001) at 594.

52 Sweden, Press and Information Department, Ministry for Foreign Affairs, *Swedish Election Guide 2002* (Edita Norstedts Trykeri, Stockholm, 2002) at 18, available online at <http://www.utrikes.regeringen.se/inenglish/projects/election_guide/> (date accessed: 15 January 2004). The threshold of 8 percent reflects a desire to minimize the ability of a candidate with little support from leapfrogging up the party list. However, this is an arbitrary decision, and it is therefore possible that a different threshold could be established in Canada.

53 In Belgium, for example, the threshold that candidates must meet is established through a formula that adds together the number of party votes and individual votes, and then divides this figure by the number of list seats allocated to the party, plus one. The results of this formula are then used to allocate seats. Another option could be to award list seats to candidates who receive the largest number of individual votes. In this instance, all party votes would be treated as votes for the party with no preference for list candidates. Candidates therefore receiving any individual votes would be ranked based on the number of votes, and list seats would be distributed accordingly.

54 See, Canada, Royal Commission on Electoral Reform and Party Financing, *Final Report Volume 1: Reforming Electoral Democracy* (Ottawa: Minister of Supply and Services, 1991) at 99–122.

55 *Ibid.* at Chapter 3, at 269.

56 T. Arseneau, "Electing Representative Legislatures: Lessons from New Zealand," in H. Milner ed., *Making Every Vote Count: Reassessing Canada's Electoral System* (Peterborough: Broadview Press, 1999) at 135.

57 N. Watt, "Women win half of Welsh seats," *The Guardian*, Saturday, 3 May 2003. Online: <http://www.politics.guardian.co.uk/wales/story/0,9061,948680,00.html> (date accessed: 23 January 2004).

58 T. Arseneau, "The Representation of Women Under PR: Lessons from New Zealand" (November 1997) *Policy Options* at 12.

59 Canada, Royal Commission on Electoral Reform and Party Financing, *Final Report Volume 1: Reforming Electoral Democracy* (Ottawa: Minister of Supply and Services, 1991) at Chapter 3, at 270.

60 *Ibid.* at 272. The Lortie Commission suggested this reimbursement be "equal to the percentage of that party's representation of women." The example provided by Lortie was a party with 25 percent women would be eligible for a 125 percent reimbursement, up to a maximum of 150 per cent.

61 *Ibid.* at 272–273.

62 The International Institute for Democracy and Electoral Assistance, "Global Database of Quotas for Women," online: <http://www.idea.int/quota/index.cfm> (date accessed: 23 January 2004).

63 See, The International Institute for Democracy and Electoral Assistance, *ibid.*

64 *Women's Representation in the House of Commons – vox populis*, co-organized by the University of Ottawa Research Centre on Women and Politics and the Law Commission of Canada was held on 31 October 2003 at the University of Ottawa.

65 Canada, Royal Commission on Electoral Reform and Party Financing, *Final Report Volume 1: Reforming Electoral Democracy* (Ottawa: Minister of Supply and Services, 1991) at 102.

66 See, for example, J. Pammett and L. LeDuc, "Confronting the Problem of Declining Voter Turnout Among Youth" (July 2003) 5:2 *Electoral Insight*; E. Gidengil, A. Blais, N. Nevitte and R. Nadeau, "Turned Off or Tuned Out? Youth Participation in Politics" (2003) 5:2 *Electoral Insight*.

67 Elections Canada Press Release and Media Advisory (21 March 2003) online: <http://www.elections.ca/content.asp?section=med&document=index&dir=pre&lang=e&textonly=false> (date accessed: 19 December 2003).

68 Elections Canada, National Forum on Youth Voting (30–31 October 2003), Report, online: <http://www.elections.ca/content.asp?section=med&document=rep&dir=eveyou/forum&lang=e&textonly=false> (date accessed: 24 February 2004). Also see, Elections Canada Press Release and Media Advisory (30 October 2003) online: <http://www.elections.ca/content.asp?section=med&document=index&dir=pre&lang=e&textonly=false> (date accessed: 19 December 2003). Further to Elections Canada's work, the House of Commons recently passed a motion that directs Elections Canada to further develop its efforts in dealing with

youth electoral participation, and work proactively with various community-based youth groups. See, Motion No. 398 (17 February 2004), 37th Parliament, 3rd Session, Edited Hansard, Number 012.

[69] Information for this section is taken largely from, J. Schmidt, *Aboriginal Representation in Government: A Comparative Examination* (Ottawa: Law Commission of Canada, 2003).

[70] For a brief overview of these conflicts, see D. Keenan, *The New Zealand Wars*, online: <http://www.newzealandwars.co.nz> (date accessed: 19 December 2003).

[71] P. Niemczak, *Aboriginal Political Representation: A Review of Several Jurisdictions* (Ottawa: Library of Parliament, Research Branch, 1994) at 5.

[72] Elections New Zealand, "Maori and the Vote," online: <http://www.elections.org.nz/elections/pandr/vote/maori-seats.html> (date accessed: 19 December 2003) Voters registering for the first time can also participate in the Maori Electoral Option, even if they register between censuses.

[73] F. Barker, et al. "An Initial Assessment of the Consequences of MMP in New Zealand," in M. Shugart and M. Wattenberg, eds., *Mixed Member Electoral Systems* (New York: Oxford University Press, 2001) at 318.

[74] Niemczak, *Aboriginal Representation: A Review of Several Jurisdictions* (Ottawa: Library of Parliament, Research Branch) at 8.

[75] *Ibid.*

[76] D. Pond, "Guaranteed Aboriginal Seats in Legislatures." *Current Issue Paper #127* (Toronto: Legislative Research Service, 1992) at 14.

[77] Canada, Royal Commission On Electoral Reform and Party Financing, *Final Report Volume I: Reforming Electoral Democracy* (Ottawa: Minister of Supply and Services, 1991) at vol. I: 169–93; vol. II: 139-50; vol. IV: 229–96. See also some of the research studies done for the Commission: A. Fleras, "Aboriginal Electoral Districts for Canada: Lessons from New Zealand" in Robert Milen, ed., *Aboriginal Peoples and Electoral Reform in Canada* (Toronto: Dundurn Press, 1991) Volume 9 of the Research Studies for the Royal Commission On Electoral Reform and Party Financing, at 67–104 and R. Gibbins, "Electoral Reform and Canada's Aboriginal Population: An Assessment of Aboriginal Electoral Districts" in Robert Milen, ed., *Aboriginal Peoples and Electoral Reform in Canada* (Toronto: Dundurn Press, 1991) Volume 9 of the Research Studies for the Royal Commission On Electoral Reform and Party Financing, at

153–84. For additional research on this question, see Canada, Committee for Aboriginal Electoral Reform, *The Path to Electoral Equality* (Ottawa, 1989); L. Marchand, "Proportional Representation for Native Peoples" (1990) 13:3 *Canadian Parliamentary Review* 9; T. Schouls, "Aboriginal Peoples and Electoral Reform in Canada: Differentiated Representation versus Voter Equality" (1996) 29 *Canadian Journal of Political Science*; T. Knight "Unconstitutional Democracy? A Charter Challenge to Canada's Electoral System" (2001) 57:1 *University of Toronto Faculty Law Review* at 1–41.

78 Canada, Royal Commission on Electoral Reform and Party Financing, *supra* note 77 at vol. IV: 229–96. There are also other options for addressing Aboriginal representation within the current electoral system. For example, the Federal Elections Boundaries Commission for New Brunswick initially proposed the creation of a single electoral district in that province that would group all "Indian reserves in one electoral district." They proposed this option would allow "the currently dispersed communities to interface with only one MP instead of several as is currently the case. It would also give strength to these communities because their numbers would no longer be fragmented." See, Federal Elections Boundaries Commission for New Brunswick, *Proposed Boundaries*, online: <http://www.elections.ca/scripts/fedrep/newbruns/proposals/boundaries_e.htm> (date accessed: 3 March 2004).

79 *Ibid.* at vol. I, 176–78, 185–92.

80 *Ibid.* at 177.

81 *Ibid.* at 176.

82 *Ibid.* at 177. (Emphasis added.)

83 *Ibid.* at 189.

84 *Ibid.* at 186–87.

85 Data on Aboriginal population in the provinces and territories available from Statistics Canada, online: <http://www.statcan.ca/english/Pgdb/demo38a.htm> (date accessed: 22 October 2003).

86 The provincial electoral quotient for Quebec for the 2001 census is 96,500 and 85 percent of this figure is 82,025. This is just slightly larger than the Aboriginal population of 80,025.

87 Canada, *Report of the Royal Commission on Aboriginal Peoples: Restructuring the Relationship*, vol. 2 (Ottawa: Supply and Services Canada, 1996) at 377. (Emphasis added.)

88 *Ibid.* at 379–80.

89 *Ibid.* at 377–78. The Royal Commission on Aboriginal People was quite clear, as were the other groups that recommended AED creation, that the House of First Peoples should not be viewed as a substitute for Aboriginal self-government.

90 *Ibid.* at 381.

91 United Kingdom, Independent Commission on the Voting System, *supra* note 43 at Recommendation 9.

92 See, *Figueroa v. Canada* (Attorney General), [2003] 1 S.C.R., No.28194 (S.C.C).

93 Shugart and Wattenberg, *supra* note 51 at 594.

94 Some researchers have suggested that if it is true that double inclusion improves the chances of election, then "its selective use for under-represented groups could enhance the representativeness of the legislature. While the rules could determine whether all of none of the candidates could stand in both constituency and lists seats, a more selective application could allow for only certain candidates (e.g., women or minority group candidates) to stand in both constituency and list seats. Politics that prioritize continuity could offer dual candidacy for incumbents while a desire for renewal could secure dual candidacy for first-time candidates." A. Henderson, "Practical Consequences of Electoral Reform: International Lessons." 25 June 2002, paper presented to the Annual Meeting of the Canadian Association of Law Teachers, Toronto at 17.

Chapter 5   Implications of Adding an Element of Proportionality to Canada's Electoral System

5.1 Introduction

Previous chapters illustrated some of the potential benefits of adding an element of proportionality to Canada's electoral system.

- It would be markedly fairer than our existing first-past-the-post system, because it would reduce the discrepancy between a party's share of the seats in the House of Commons and its share of the votes.

- It would lead to the inclusion in the House of Commons of new and previously under-represented voices, such as smaller political parties.

- It would almost certainly lead to the election of greater numbers of minority and women candidates.

- It could encourage inter-party cooperation through coalition governments.

- It would reduce the huge disparities in the value of votes that currently exist in our first-past-the-post system, in which a vote for the winning party is often three to four times more "valuable" than a vote for any of the other parties.

- It would reduce the number of disregarded votes, and thus lead to an increase in the extent of "sincere," as opposed to strategic voting.

- It would produce more regionally balanced party caucuses.

- It might result in higher voter turnout.[1]

It is important to acknowledge that these are only *possible* benefits of a more proportional electoral system. To avoid creating unreasonable expectations among Canadian citizens—which could all too easily lead to disappointment and heightened disillusionment with the political system—then electoral reform must not be treated as a panacea for our present democratic malaise.

> "We believe that there are two fundamental reasons for supporting the introduction of proportional representation. The first is the advantage for all Canadians of having the Parliament of Canada reflect in broad terms the votes cast for the different parties in the election. The second is that with a proportional representation system whichever party forms the government either alone or with support of another party is more likely to have within it caucus representatives from all the regions of Canada. The first-past-the-post system (FPTP) not only tends to under-represent some points of view but it also has tended to encourage parties to be regional representatives in Parliament rather than national."
>
> K.V. Georgetti, President, Canadian Labour Congress. Submission to the Law Commission of Canada. (Received: 7 March 2003.)

It is also essential that Canadians understand the possible implications of adding an element of proportionality to the electoral system. Chapter 5 examines the potential impact of electoral reform on government stability and effectiveness, on Canadian regionalism and national unity, on Members of Parliament (particularly regarding the issue of creating two different classes of representatives), on the public services, and on government accountability. There is also a discussion of a possible increase in administrative costs.

5.2 The Impact of Minority or Coalition Governments on Political Decision Making

Single-party majority governments would occur infrequently under a mixed member proportional electoral system. In the 2000 federal election, for example, in which the Liberals parlayed just under 41 percent of the popular vote into 172 seats (57 percent of the total), our preferred mixed member proportional system would have given them only 144 seats, or 47.4 percent of the total.[2] Only when a winning party obtains more than 50 percent of the popular vote would a single-party majority government be most likely to occur. In Canada, parties have obtained such outright majorities of the vote on only five occasions since 1921.[3]

We can draw on both domestic and international experiences with minority and coalition governments to assess the claim that a mixed member proportional system will lead inevitably to greater instability and less effective governance. Dobell notes that there have been nine minority governments at the federal level since Confederation, the most recent being the short-lived government of Joe Clark in 1979.[4] On average, these minority governments have lasted for a bit less than 20 months, compared to more than 50 months for majority governments.[5] In six of the nine cases, however, the governments fell at the initiative of the sitting prime minister and his party, who calculated that they could win a legislative majority in an ensuing election.[6]

Canadians have much less experience with coalition governments in which members of different political parties are brought into the cabinet. At the federal level, the only example is the Unionist coalition under Prime Minister Robert Borden (1917–20). Provincially, there have been coalition governments in Ontario (United Farmers and Labour, 1919–23), British Columbia (Liberals and Conservatives, 1941–52), Saskatchewan (a "Tory-dominated 'Cooperative' coalition" from 1929 to 1934) and Manitoba, during Bracken's lengthy tenure in office from 1922 to 1942.[7] International experience, however, suggests that "[c]oalitions are inherently more fragile than single-party governments and are more likely to break up during the life of a parliament or to lead to early elections."[8]

"Our experience with minority governments ... strongly suggests that if these become the norm under a PR system, governments would be less durable ... It is difficult to gauge how Canadians would react to this new pattern of parliamentary politics. Criticisms have been voiced in recent decades about governments having too much power, the executive dominating Parliament and the prime minister behaving like an elected monarch. PR would likely make governments more fragile, but this may be what Canadians actually want, especially if it means governments are more willing to listen and compromise. It is striking that Australia, the country where the working of the Westminster model arouses the least opposition, is also the only one where the power of the ruling party or coalition is checked by a PR-elected second chamber rarely controlled by the government party or coalition."

L. Massicotte, "Changing the Canadian Electoral System" (February 2001)
Choices: Strengthening Canadian Democracy 7:1 at 15.

In short, adopting a mixed member proportional system would likely result in somewhat shorter-lived governments. Nonetheless, it would be a misnomer to use the word "unstable" to characterize this situation. Governments formed on the basis of proportional representation elections in the Scandinavian countries and Germany, as well as New Zealand and Scotland since their adoption of mixed member proportional systems, have exhibited quite satisfactory levels of political stability, if one measures this in terms of the length of time a particular cabinet stays in power.

More importantly, the durability of cabinets and the length in office of governments do not appear to be strongly related to effectiveness of policy making. Conventional wisdom used to be that single-party governments were more effective decision makers than minority or coalition governments. This was thought to be especially true in the realm of economic policy, where a strong governing majority would in theory be able to use its legislative superiority to enact policies that might be unpopular in the short term but absolutely necessary for a nation's future competitiveness. Coalition governments might not be able to make these tough but necessary decisions, since junior partners in these administrations would be more likely to precipitate an early election than to accept the political fallout from highly unpopular policies.

In the past decade or so, research has called into question this traditional belief.[9] Recent research, for example, examines 36 established democracies, dividing them into two basic categories: majoritarian democracies (with strong executives, first-past-the-post electoral systems, and single-party governments) and consensus democracies (with proportional representation electoral systems, coalition governments, and comparatively weak executives). Results indicate that since 1970 the rate of economic growth in countries with majoritarian systems has not been significantly higher than that of countries with consensus-based systems (including some form of proportional representation).[10] On a number of other economic indicators—such as inflation, unemployment, strike activity and budget deficits—the consensus democracies have actually performed better than the majoritarian countries since 1970, though the differences between the two groups were usually modest. The sole exception is inflation, where the consensus democracies have an advantage over their majoritarian counterparts.[11]

One can go even further and argue that countries with some form of proportional representation—the so-called consensus democracies—have an advantage in economic performance over majoritarian systems. This is because first-past-the-post systems are likely to promote a regular alternation in and out of power of political parties that are ideologically polarized. These parties are frequently tempted to undo or radically alter the economic policies of their predecessors, as was seen in Ontario, for instance, with the transition from Bob Rae's New Democratic government to that of Mike Harris' Conservative government in 1995. This can inhibit the ability of policy makers to engage in long-term economic planning. By contrast, "broad proportional representation coalition governments help engender a stability and coherence in decision-making which allows for national development."[12]

5.3 Regionalism

Some sceptics worry that a mixed member proportional system "would almost certainly stimulate regionally oriented parties, especially in a dramatically transformed party system where regional parties might be logical coalition partners for larger nation-wide parties."[13] In Chapter 4 it was recommended that Canada adopt a mixed member proportional system with compensation seats awarded at the provincial level. One of the objectives in doing so was precisely to even out the regional imbalances in party caucuses created by the current electoral system. Another important objective was the desire to establish lists of candidates for the compensatory seats. The preferred electoral formula might well make it easier for regionalist or autonomist parties to elect candidates to the House of Commons. In Alberta, for instance, had the recommended electoral system been in place for the 2000 federal election, a western separatist party would have required approximately 50,000 votes (4 percent of the total) in order to win a seat in the House of Commons. In British Columbia, a similar number of votes (50,000, or 3 percent of the total) would have qualified a party for one compensation seat in Parliament.

To some observers, this raises the specter of small separatist (or other extremist) parties holding the country to ransom, trying to extract policy concessions in exchange for their participation in a coalition government.[14] This cannot be excluded as a possible consequence of electoral reform. It does not seem a likely outcome, however. If one examines the simulated results of the 2000 election under Scottish-style model (see table 10), the New Democratic Party would have gained one compensation seat in Alberta with 5.4 percent of the vote, while the Progressive Conservatives would have been awarded two list seats on the basis of just under 14 percent of the vote. Thus while smaller parties will find it easier to elect at least one member to the House of Commons under the proposed version of mixed member proportional system, a separatist or any other "protest" party would have to win considerably more than 15 percent of the popular vote *in more than one province* to gain significant representation in Parliament. If a separatist party were able to achieve this level of electoral support, it might well be able to make inroads even in a first-past-the-post system, especially if its support were regionally concentrated.

In addition, we should point out that the electoral transition of 1993, which signaled the rise to national prominence of two powerful regional opposition parties, the Bloc Québécois and the Reform Party (which became the Canadian Alliance Party), occurred in large part because the first-past-the-post electoral system, with its two dominant parties, appeared unable to accommodate the pressures of regionalism. Admittedly, the size and number of regional parties could possibly increase under a mixed member proportional system. It is at least arguable, however, that it is better to have these regionalist parties represented in Parliament with a handful of seats among them than to try to rely on an electoral system that systematically discriminates against minor parties. The latter option seems to be a formula for voter discontent and alienation.

5.4 Two "Classes" of Representatives

One of the most frequently voiced criticisms of a mixed member proportional electoral systems is that they tend to create two different classes of representatives, one elected through the frequently cut-throat realm of constituency politics, the other on the basis of their positioning on party lists. Interestingly, observers differ on which category constitutes the subordinate class. According to one electoral observer, "there would be no doubt that the Members of Parliament filling the compensation seats would be second-class citizens."[15] Others, however, are convinced that the Members of Parliament elected by proportional representation would form a kind of legislative aristocracy: freed from constituency duties and the need to ensure their personal re-election, these representatives would have time to devote to "higher-order" pursuits, such as policy formulation and long-term strategic planning for their party as a whole. The Jenkins Report also notes that list Members of Parliament might establish themselves as "shadow" Members of Parliament in constituencies where they were contemplating seeking a party nomination in the hope of becoming a directly elected constituency

Member of Parliament. In this case, the list Members of Parliament would have a considerable advantage over their constituency rivals, in that they would have fewer constraints on their time to keep them from wooing the voters in the riding. In the view of the Jenkins commission, this situation would be "inimical to the best traditions of a Member of Parliament performing at least a semi-impartial role in his or her constituency between elections and endeavoring to serve all constituents—those who supported him or her and those who did not—with equal diligence. If there is a rival and equally active Member of Parliament of an opposing party on the scene this link is almost inevitably weakened if not broken."[16] Critics of mixed member proportional electoral systems believe that this functional hierarchy of Members of Parliament could foster jealousy and competition between the two groups, possibly crippling Parliament as an effective decision-making body.

These perceptions about mixed member proportional systems are sufficiently widespread that they need to be addressed by advocates of a different model. Fortunately, the recent experiences of a number of countries and regions (Germany, New Zealand, Scotland, and Wales, most notably) allow an assessment of whether these criticisms are based on exaggerated fears or whether they have some basis in fact. It is interesting to note that the Jenkins Report, which discusses in some detail the notion that two classes of Members of Parliament are created in a mixed electoral system, ultimately concludes that this is not a "formidable" problem and does not represent as much of a departure from the Westminster model as is often assumed.

In New Zealand, the Royal Commission on the Electoral System observed that the operation of mixed member proportional electoral system in what was then West Germany "does not appear to have weakened party unity or discipline or to have led to two distinct classes of Members of Parliament."[17] Other electoral system observers concur and suggest that the argument that it creates two classes of warring Members of Parliament is based more on perception than reality: "in the two dozen countries with mixed systems, no tensions [between the two categories of representatives] are reported. In New Zealand, however, proportional representation members are *perceived* by some to

"In the first place [having two different types of MPs] is not really such a break with the British tradition as may superficially be thought. Throughout the nineteenth century there was a considerable difference of category between county and borough members. In addition the Scottish and Irish members were mostly elected on a different franchise from the English and Welsh ones. And some constituencies were always regarded, at any rate by some politicians, as having a greater prestige than others. Some saw the City of London as being peculiarly appropriate for great financiers or, on two occasions, for party leaders, and Lord Randolph Churchill several times tried to escape from what he regarded as the mediocrity of South Paddington to the romance of a 'great industrial borough.' The university seats, different both in electorate and in electoral method, persisted until 1950. And we are about to move into a position in which some MPs will represent areas with devolution and hence will have more restricted constituency duties. Furthermore, there has long been a difference of practice, if not of theory, between those who entered Parliament primarily to seek a national role, often switching from one constituency to an utterly disparate one in order to achieve it, and those who sprang out of a particular locality, found their greatest satisfaction in representing and serving it, and could not easily have been imagined, by themselves or others, as migrating to a seat in a different part of the country."

United Kingdom, Independent Commission on the Voting System [Jenkins Commission], *Final Report* (1998) at paragraph 115.

be 'second-class' Members of Parliament, though in practice there is little to substantiate that perception."[18]

In one detailed study, the author found that all list Members of Parliament in New Zealand have been assigned to at least one constituency, and some have "begun identifying themselves as the point of contact in their assigned electorate(s) for their party."[19] The author also notes that voters in Germany tend to approach both constituency and list Members of Parliament for assistance with specific requests or complaints. The choice of which Member of Parliament to approach appears to be determined at least in part by the party identification or affiliation of the voter in question.[20]

A mixed electoral system, at the very least, creates the potential for conflict between the directly elected constituency Member of Parliament and his or her "shadow" list Member of Parliament, and can confuse voters about the roles and duties of each representative. Directly elected representatives will undoubtedly resent being undermined by list Members of Parliament, some of whom they might have actually defeated at the polls. Although time and experience with a new system may allow, as in Germany, for developing traditions of cooperation between Members of Parliament, it may be helpful to facilitate the transition in electoral system by establishing protocols, in particular with respect to the duty for list Members of Parliament to inform constituency Members of Parliament when representing constituents. For these reasons, the Commission puts forward these recommendations:

Recommendation 16

Provincial and territorial list Members of Parliament should have all the rights and privileges of constituency Members of Parliament.

Recommendation 17

Parties represented in the House of Commons should develop protocols for ensuring the effective co-functioning of constituency and list Members of Parliament, including consideration of methods for informing constituency Members of Parliament of issues or cases being taken up by list Members of Parliament.

There is no doubt that the adoption of a mixed member proportional electoral system would entail a departure from the traditional mores of parliamentary life in this country. There would inevitably need to be a period of adaptation to the new system, and conscious effort on the part of political parties and Members of Parliament to smooth over any differences that might arise between the two groups of Members of Parliament. Nevertheless, recent experiences in Germany, New Zealand, and elsewhere suggest that the new system would not involve as radical a change from the status quo as some of its critics have suggested.

"...analysis and discussion has demonstrated the similarity between electorate and list MPs: their constitutional positions are the same; socially and politically they resemble one another quite closely; and there is little difference in their roles except in some aspects of constituency work ... The only major difference between the electorate and list MPs is with their modes of election. This difference, however, has proven to be a very significant one. Given New Zealand's traditional attachment to single-member constituencies, it has proven very difficult for a new political culture to evolve that is understood and accepted by citizens and elite alike ... [T]he fact that the newer parties are much more reliant than the older parties on list MP representation means that they are particularly vulnerable to the negative perceptions associated with 'second-class' MPs. These problems may resolve themselves in time if the MMP electoral system continues. As the data ... demonstrate, *the problem is less one of reality than of inaccurate perception, for the list MPs are at least as well qualified as the constituency MPs to perform the normal tasks of political representation.*"

L.J. Ward, "'Second-Class MPs'? New Zealand's Adaptation to Mixed-Member Parliamentary Representation" (1998) 49:2 *Political Science* at 142–43.

The issue of how to conduct by-elections for the two different types of Members of Parliament must also be addressed. In Germany, there are no by-elections: politicians who resign, retire, or die while in office are replaced by the candidate who was ranked next highest on their party list for the Land in question. It has been argued that holding by-elections to replace directly-elected representatives would create perverse incentives in the system: "A party would not be able to guarantee that it would win the by-election. Therefore, the rational strategy for parties under such a scheme would be to maximize the number of list seats it seeks to win in elections and minimize its constituency seats."[21]

This seems a dubious proposition for a mixed member proportional system in Canada, and it does not appear that holding by-elections to replace only the directly elected Members of Parliament has had any negative effect in either New Zealand or Scotland, where the practice is common.

Recommendation 18

Vacancies in the directly-elected (constituency) portion of Members of Parliament should be filled by means of a by-election, while vacancies among list Members of Parliament should be filled by the candidate who was ranked next highest on the party list for the province or territory in question.

Finally, there is another potential political problem that might arise from the difference in the way the two types of Members of Parliament are elected to the House of Commons. What happens in the event that a list Member of Parliament defects from his or her party and decides to sit in Parliament as an independent or to join another party? List Members of Parliament are elected because of their party affiliation, so is there a reason to worry? This issue was resolved in New Zealand and should be debated in Canada.[22]

5.5 Government Formation and Accountability

In a first-past-the-post electoral system it is quite rare for there to be any uncertainty about the identity of the governing party once an election has taken place. Only when no single party succeeds in winning a majority of the seats in parliament does any negotiation take place to determine who will have the opportunity to govern. This can lead to some mildly surprising results, as happened in Ontario after the 1985 provincial election. In this case the second-place finisher, the Liberals, negotiated a formal accord with the third-place New Democratic Party, in which the latter pledged its legislative support for a Liberal government in exchange for the enactment of some of its key policy priorities.

Elections in proportional representation systems (including mixed member proportional systems), by contrast, can be followed by protracted negotiations among potential coalition partners, leading to agreements that surprise, disappoint, or even anger voters. Such was the case in the first mixed member proportional election in New Zealand, held in 1996. The four largest parties in New Zealand at the time of the election were the governing National Party, Labour (the principal opposition party), the Alliance, and New Zealand First.[23] Throughout the campaign, New Zealand First and its leader, Winston Peters, had made it quite clear that they were most likely to ally them-selves with Labour in a possible coalition government. After the election,[24] and nearly two months of negotiations, National and New Zealand First formed a coalition government. Many of the latter party's supporters felt betrayed.[25]

This sort of perverse deal making is a risk in a proportional representation system. However, even in a proportional representation system voters often have the ultimate means to punish parties that they feel stray too far from their electoral promises. In the instance cited, New Zealand First suffered considerable losses in the 1999 election (it was reduced to five seats), which served as a warning to other politi-cians who might be tempted to imitate Winston Peters' somewhat "slippery" behaviour.[26]

Political parties in Canada would have to reflect seriously on the process of forming coalitions under a mixed member proportional system. Parties will have to carefully consider the ways in which they form coalitions, both before and after each election. This would include keeping voters informed of the nature and extent of coalition negotiations (both pre- and post-election), and how different parties might work together if or when they form the government. Parties should enter into coalition discussions with the understanding that voters will have the ultimate say in terms of satisfaction with the coalitions that are formed. Coalitions that are formed without voter knowledge or support would not only contribute to citizen dissatisfaction with the system of democratic governance, but would possibly provide voters with reason to vote differently in the next election.

5.6 Administrative Costs

There would be some one-time costs associated with implementing a mixed member proportional system. For example, there would be costs associated with establishing education campaigns or a referendum. Once adopted, there would be further costs: redrawing electoral boundaries, developing compensation seats (including the addition of three compensation seats for the territories), establishing special Aboriginal seats in the House of Commons or a House of Aboriginal People, reviewing relevant policies and legislation, devising new election ballots, and so on. Political parties would have to adapt their internal organizations and procedures.

The International Institute for Democracy and Electoral Assistance estimates that only a two-round system is likely to place more of a burden on a country's electoral administration machinery than a mixed member proportional system.[27] Nevertheless, the Commission concurs with the New Zealand Royal Commission on the Electoral System, which stated, "the administrative costs of operating a mixed member proportional system would not be greatly different from the cost of operating a plurality system *with relatively the same number of Members of Parliament.* We therefore do not see the cost of introducing Mixed Member Proportional as a factor of any great significance."[28]

5.7 Impact on the Public Service

Introducing an element of proportionality into Canada's voting system would undoubtedly have some implications for the public service. The transition could create challenges, such as preparing public servants and the new government for a different type of transition period, and learning the different political dynamics that result from coalition and minority governments. Compared to the first-past-the-post system, the transition from one government to another might take longer, especially if the election produces a minority government, followed by a period of negotiation to form a ruling coalition.

There could also be changes in how parliamentary committees operate. For example, more diverse and inclusive committees might result in more frequent and detailed requests for research and information from the public service. Likewise, "under a minority government ministers would need to undertake extensive consultations with non-government parties on a wide range of policy initiatives in order to secure the necessary support to pass legislation."[29] Further, initial mixed member proportional elections might result in a large number of new and inexperienced members of a legislature or Members of Parliament, creating new responsibilities for public servants,[30] although similar dynamics can also unfold within the first-past-the-post system.

For the most part, however, there is no reason to believe that the public service would not be able to serve well under such a system. Within the context of the existing first-past-the-post system, the public service has successfully assisted with numerous transitions of ideologically different governments, most recently when the Liberal Party won a majority government over the incumbent Progressive

"The evidence … [in New Zealand] … indicates that the impact of MMP on the day-to-day functioning of the public service has been relatively slight and certainly considerably less than some had anticipated. For example, there have been no fundamental changes in the operations of the executive or in the relationship between the executive and parliament … In brief, continuity rather than change has been the predominant feature of the new MMP environment, at least in relation to the nation's key political institutions."

J. Boston, S. Levine, E. McLeay, N.S. Roberts and H. Schmidt, "The Impact of Electoral Reform on the Public Service: The New Zealand Case" (1998) 57:3 *Australian Journal of Public Administration* at 73.

Conservatives in 1993. In addition, it would not alter the existing role of the cabinet in government, "…with cabinet (and its committees) remaining as the highest decision-making authority and ministers still being bound by the doctrines of individual and collective ministerial responsibility."[31] Overall, there is no reason to believe that introducing an element of proportionality into the existing electoral system would fundamentally challenge the ability of the public service to maintain an effective system of governance.

5.8 Conclusion: Setting the Bar for Electoral Reform

Opponents of electoral reform in Canada are quite correct to point out that no electoral system is neutral.[32] The essential question is whether its strengths outweigh its disadvantages, and whether *on the whole* a new system would help to achieve more of the democratic values outlined in Chapter 3 than our first-past-the-post system currently does. In other words, a reasonable bar must be set for the advocates of electoral reform to prove their case; all too often in the past, the opponents of change have seemed to demand that uncertainty about the possible impact of reform be reduced to zero.

This Chapter has listed some of the possible implications of adopting a mixed member proportional electoral system. Coalition governments would likely become the norm, but coalitions might actually be a positive feature of reform. By helping to constrain executive power, coalition governments can increase consensus-making, consultation, and government responsiveness (though this is not automatically the case). The experience of countries like Germany and New Zealand (even though its experience is limited) suggests that the fear of destabilizing consequences is overblown.

Regional parties would find the barriers to representation lowered, but the comparatively small number of compensation seats in each province would tend to limit their size and influence. While two groups of Members of Parliament would exist in the House of Commons, experience elsewhere does not confirm the belief that they would become warring classes. Moreover, the parties themselves can undertake measures to prevent any factionalism. Finally, although the ability of voters to hold governing parties accountable for their actions is attenuated somewhat under proportional representation, the experience of New Zealand and other countries indicates that voters still retain the ultimate power to reward or punish incumbent parties.

The potential drawbacks need to be set against the likely or possible benefits that were previously outlined. The new system would be fairer; it would be more representative of our society; it would be more inclusive (in terms of smaller parties); it would reduce the number of disregarded votes; and it would make party caucuses in the House of Commons more representative of the various regions in the country. It could also help to increase voter turnout. For these reasons, a mixed member proportional electoral system meets, and indeed surpasses, any *realistic* test for proving the desirability of reform.

---

1   For a discussion of the possible benefits and drawbacks of adopting a mixed member proportional system in Canada, see L. Massicotte, "Changing the Canadian Electoral System" (2001) 7:1 *Choices: Strengthening Canadian Democracy.*

2   These "simulated" results must be interpreted with caution, since they assume that the results in constituency elections would have been the same no matter what electoral system, first-past-the-post or mixed member proportional, was in place. Of course, as most advocates of mixed member proportional point out, a new system would alter the calculations of individual voters, and make it less likely that anomalous results, such as the Liberals sweeping 98 percent or 99 percent of the seats in Ontario, would occur. For a discussion of this topic, see H. Milner, "The Case for Proportional Representation in Canada" in H. Milner ed., *Making Every Vote Count: Reassessing Canada's Electoral System* (Peterborough: Broadview Press, 1999) at 39–40.

3   We choose 1921 as the point of departure since it marks the birth of the modern multi-party (or, more accurately, the two-party plus) system in Canada. A party won at least 50 percent of the popular vote in the federal elections of 1940 (Liberals, 52 percent), 1949 (Liberals, 50 percent), 1953 (Liberals, 50 percent), 1958 (Progressive Conservatives, 54 percent), and 1984 (Progressive Conservatives, 50 percent).

4 P. Dobell, "What Could Canadians Expect from a Minority Government?" (2000) 1:6 *Policy Matters* at 4–10.

5 Massicotte, *supra* note 1 at 14.

6 Dobell, *supra* note 4 at 9.

7 Massicotte, *supra* note 1 at 14.

8 *Ibid.* at 15.

9 *Ibid.* at 17.

10 Lijphart acknowledges that the majoritarian democracies (United States, United Kingdom, Canada etc.) have a slight advantage over the consensus democracies in terms of annual economic growth, but the difference is not statistically significant. A. Lijphart, *Patterns of Democracy: Government Forms and Performance in Thirty-Six Countries* (New Haven: Yale University Press, 1999) at 265.

11 *Ibid.*

12 A. Reynolds and B. Reilly, *The International IDEA Handbook of Electoral System Design*, 2nd ed. (Stockholm: International Institute for Democracy and Electoral Assistance, 1997) at 63.

13 K. Weaver, "MMP is Too Much of Some Good Things" in H. Milner ed., *Making Every Vote Count* (Peterborough: Broadview Press, 1999) at 80.

14 Courtney warns that "[I]n its extreme, [a reformed electoral system] could lead, as purely proportional schemes such as Israel's have, to a party system composed of a variety of competing regional, linguistic, religious or ethnic factions, none of whom could, on its own, construct a majority government. The implications for Canadian national unity could be profound." J. Courtney, "Electoral Reform and Canada's Parties" in H. Milner ed., *Making Every Vote Count: Reassessing Canada's Electoral System* (Peterborough: Broadview Press, 1999) at 98.

15 R. Katz, "Electoral Reform is not as Simple as it Looks" in H. Milner ed., *Making Every Vote Count: Reassessing Canada's Electoral System* (Peterborough: Broadview Press, 1999) at 106.

16 United Kingdom, Independent Commission on the Voting System [Jenkins Commission]. Final Report (1998) at para 116. This has occurred in the Scottish Parliament, prompting some directly elected MPs to complain about their list counterparts "poaching" on their territory. See A. Henderson, "Practical Consequences of Electoral Reform" (25 June 2002) Paper presented

to the Annual Meeting of the Canadian Association of Law Teachers, Toronto at 15.

17 New Zealand, Royal Commission on the Electoral System. *Towards a Better Democracy* (Wellington: Government Printer, 1986) at 61.

18 Massicotte, *supra* note 1 at 13. (Emphasis added.)

19 L.J. Ward, "'Second-Class MPs'? New Zealand's Adaptation to Mixed-Member Parliamentary Representation" (1998) 49:2 Political Science at 137.

20 *Ibid.*

21 D.M. Farrell, *Comparing Electoral Systems* (London: Prentice Hall, 1997) at 98.

22 This issue became salient in New Zealand in 1997, when Alamein Kopu, a list Member of Parliament for the Alliance, resigned from her party to sit as an "Independent Maori Member of Parliament." The Alliance argued that Kopu should have been forced to resign her seat, especially since she, along with all other Alliance list candidates, had signed a written pledge to resign from Parliament in the event she left the party. Eventually, the New Zealand Parliament's Privileges Committee ruled that Kopu did not have to resign her seat and could continue to sit as an independent. This generated considerable controversy and raised questions about the legitimacy of Kopu's actions. This case is described in detail in Ward, *supra* note 19 at 140–42.

23 The New Zealand legislature in 1996, elected three years earlier on the basis of first-past-the-post, contained 99 Members of Parliament. The Alliance, with two Members of Parliament, had won over 18 percent of the vote in 1993, while New Zealand First, also with 2 seats, had won only 8 percent of the vote. The parliament was enlarged to 120 seats for the first MMP election in 1996.

24 The National Party placed first (44 seats), Labour second (37 seats), and New Zealand First came in third (17 seats).

25 F. Barker, J. Boston, S. Levine, E. McLeay, and N.S. Roberts, "An Initial Assessment of the Consequences of MMP in New Zealand" in M.S. Shugart and M.P. Wattenberg, eds., *Mixed Member Electoral Systems: The Best of Both Worlds?* (Oxford: Oxford University Press, 2001) at 301.

26 Massicotte, *supra* note 1 at 16.

27 Reynolds and Reilly, *supra* note 12 at 119.

28 New Zealand Royal Commission on the Electoral System, *supra* note 17 at 65. (Emphasis added.)

29 J. Boston, S. Levine, E. McLeay, N.S. Roberts and H. Schmidt, "The Impact of Electoral Reform on the Public Service: The New Zealand Case" (1998) *Australian Journal of Public Administration,* 57(3) at 77.

30 *Ibid.* at 74.

31 *Ibid.* at 73.

32 J. Courtney, "Is Talk of Electoral Reform Just Whistling in the Wind?" (2001) 22:6 *Policy Options* at 21.

Chapter 6 The Process of Electoral Reform— Engaging Citizens in Democratic Change

Throughout its public engagement process, the Commission heard from a broad range of citizens who expressed varying opinions about how to proceed with electoral system reform. For some there is a growing sentiment that the electoral reform question has been "studied enough" and that it is now time to act and engage in a meaningful reform process. At the same time, there were also strong beliefs that citizens should play a role in changing the voting system.

Chapter 6 explores how the proposed mixed member proportional might be implemented. How might the process of reform unfold? To answer this question, the Report draws on the results of the Commission's consultation process, and the experiences of other Canadian jurisdictions, such as Quebec, British Columbia, New Brunswick, and Prince Edward Island, as well as the experiences of other countries such as New Zealand and Italy. The reform process must include informing citizens about proposed changes and allowing them to express their points of view. It should also benefit from the insights of similar processes in Canada that are underway or already completed.

6.1 Electoral Reform and Citizen Engagement

Electoral system reform is increasingly prominent in the Canadian political landscape. British Columbia, Quebec, and Prince Edward Island, followed closely by New Brunswick and Ontario have traveled further down the road toward reform than other jurisdictions and they can offer insights about how Canadians might go about reforming their electoral system.

The government of British Columbia, which holds 77 of the 79 seats in its legislature,[1] recently introduced a Citizens' Assembly to review the existing electoral system and make recommendations for reform. This Citizens' Assembly includes individuals selected randomly from its voters' list: 20 individuals from each of the province's 79 electoral districts. The voters' list was stratified by age and gender to "ensure equal numbers of men's and women's names and reflection of the provincial age distribution 18 years and over" in the larger pool of potential candidates. The 20 citizens selected in each riding were then invited to express their interest in serving on the assembly. Final selection of two members per riding took place in late 2003–early 2004.[2] In addition to the 158 randomly selected citizens in the assembly, there are two Aboriginal members and a non-voting chair, who may appoint up to four vice-chairs to be regional back-ups at sub-panels and public hearings.[3]

With a budget of $5.5 million, the Citizens' Assembly will gather information on the various electoral systems in use throughout the world; experts from other countries will be invited to explain the operation of their systems. The Assembly will act as a kind of citizens' jury, hearing the champions of various electoral systems and recommending a smaller number (three or four options) for consideration in public hearings. An information householder, outlining these different options along with their strengths and weaknesses, will be mailed out to all voters in April 2004. In May and June of 2004, up to 30 public hearings will be held in different parts of the province; by November 2004, the Assembly will make its final recommendation. The Assembly's constitution limits it to recommending *only one electoral option*, either the status quo or an alternative. If an alternative electoral system is recommended, it will be put to a province-wide referendum at the next provincial election, scheduled for May 2005. The ballot question will be a simple "Yes" or "No" on support for the proposed system. To pass, a supermajority is required: 60 percent of voters in 60 percent of the ridings must approve.[4]

In summer 2002, the Quebec government created a steering committee for the Estates-General on the Reform of Democratic Institutions. This steering committee consisted of nine members who were drawn from politics, academia, and civil society (including organizations representing women, youth, the cultural communities, and labour). In addition, one citizen representing each of the

17 administrative districts in the province served as a secretariat for the steering committee, assisting the latter in its consultations and deliberations. According to the then-Minister Responsible for the Reform of Democratic Institutions, Jean-Pierre Charbonneau, the Quebec government's survey of electoral reform elsewhere in the world distilled three basic conditions that must be met for reforms to have any chance of success.[5]

- There must be a citizens' committee (which need not be selected randomly) that is not "in thrall" (inféodé) to the political parties, so that citizens believe that "the reforms are being made not to favour a specific party, but in the interests of the general public." [Translation]

- Political parties must be involved in the process in some way, since inevitably they will be responsible for implementing any changes.

- The citizens' committee must have as one of its primary functions the education of citizens about the stakes of electoral reform and the various options to be considered.

In addition to making several recommendations for a more open and inclusive system of governance, the "Rapport du Comité directeur des États généraux sur la réforme des institutions démocratiques" recommended adopting proportional representation for its provincial elections. The Liberal government in Quebec recently announced its intentions to introduce legislation that brings some element of proportionality into the voting system.

The recent release of the final report of Prince Edward Island's Electoral Reform Commission stands as another reminder of the growing prominence of the electoral reform question. Charged with independently exploring options for electoral reform, Prince Edward Island's Commission produced a background paper and organized detailed consultations with citizens about "the possibility of introducing some elements of proportional representation within the electoral process."[6] The Commission's final report suggests that citizens might be better served by an electoral system that incorporates some element of proportionality from, most notably, a mixed member proportional or a single transferable vote system. The Commission also recommends further consultations to determine what citizens want for an alternative to the first-past-the-post system.[7]

Despite employing slightly different approaches to electoral reform, these engagement processes share a common theme: citizens are provided with an opportunity to participate actively in various aspects of the decision-making process. The feedback and input received by the Law Commission through its citizen engagement process, and the prominence of electoral reform provincially, suggest that now is the time for Canada to adopt a different voting system. In addition to commissioning research, we co-hosted public consultations, sponsored and participated in conferences, special forums, and colloquiums, met with various groups and individuals, and invited comments and feedback via telephone, mail (both regular and e-mail), and our website. (See Appendix B for details of the public engagement strategies used.) The feedback and input that we received through this process provided the backdrop to the conclusions and recommendations within this Report. The question now becomes how to balance actually implementing a process of reform while maintaining ongoing citizen engagement. How might citizens be included in an ongoing dialogue about electoral system reform?

It is crucial that citizens be included in an ongoing dialogue about electoral system reform, and that the process of reform include a citizens' engagement strategy. Many Canadians are eager to participate in democratic governance, and they need and want information. The implementation of this strategy should not be the concern of the government alone, and should aim for a broad and diverse representation, notably including women, youth, minority groups, and citizens from all regions. It should seek the views of political parties (minority parties as well as mainstream), Parliamentarians, and citizens' groups. The engagement might proceed more smoothly if presented with one particular model of electoral reform. A draft bill outlining the Commission's proposed system would certainly facilitate discussion.

An engagement strategy requires sufficient resources and time—at least one year—to gather all viewpoints and make its recommendations. Ultimately, Elections Canada will be responsible for implementing any electoral system adopted by Parliament, including institutional changes and new administrative practices.

The question of what sort of approval is necessary for changes to the electoral system is debatable. Is it necessary to hold a referendum to change the electoral system? There is no constitutional impediment to changing the electoral system without a referendum. Indeed, in the past, electoral reforms at various levels of government in Canada have been adopted by the simple passage of legislation. More recently, in Quebec, for example, the government of Jean Charest has pledged to introduce some element of proportional representation into the system within two years of its election. Such a move would have widespread support in the electorate, since both the Parti Québécois and the Action démocratique du Québec have publicly endorsed electoral reform and the Estates-General have already conducted extensive public consultations on the issue.

While there is no single preferred or constitutionally sanctioned path for achieving electoral reform, in recent years, many Canadians have argued that voters should approve significant political or constitutional reforms. Even if electoral reform does not require constitutional changes, it is a major change in how Canadian democracy functions. Therefore, holding a referendum should be considered.

New Zealand held two referendums, the first a non-binding plebiscite to see if citizens desired change and, if so, what their preferred alternative system might be. An overwhelming majority of those who voted—almost 85 percent—were in favour of changing the electoral system, with mixed member proportional as the most preferred alternative.[8] The second referendum, held in conjunction with a general election in 1993, asked voters whether they preferred a mixed member proportional system or the status quo. Voter turnout was 85 percent and a narrow majority (54 percent to 46 percent) supported a mixed member proportional system.[9]

Two other liberal democracies reformed their electoral systems in the 1990s: Japan and Italy. In Japan, in 1988, an advisory committee was established to examine the country's electoral system; in 1990 it issued a report recommending a mixed system similar to Germany's. After a few years of negotiations, the governing coalition in Japan ultimately agreed on a parallel system, in which three-fifths of the seats in the Diet would be elected on the basis of first-past-the-post, and the rest according to proportional representation in 11 regional blocks.[10] This system was put in place for the 1996 election without a referendum.

In Italy, concerns over endemic problems in the party system instigated a referendum abrogativo to initiate change. This provision allows voters to initiate a referendum to strike down an existing law or provisions in a law if they can gather 500,000 signatures within a 90-day period. In 1991, an initial referendum was held on eliminating preference voting for the Italian lower house (the Chamber of Deputies). This passed by an overwhelming majority of 96 percent of valid votes (with a turnout of 62 percent). This launched yet another referendum drive in late 1991 that gathered 1,250,000 signatures for reform of party financing and the electoral system for Italy's upper house (the Senate). These reforms were endorsed in a second referendum in 1993.[11] According to some observers, Italy's provision for the referendum abrogativo was crucial in securing successful electoral reform, since it "allows those outside the government and the legislature to initiate change. It also produces an ongoing dialogue between the general public, those sponsoring the referenda, existing politicians, the courts ... and Parliament..."[12]

While adding a referendum to give legitimacy to a proposed reform appears attractive, it does raise a number of concerns. First, and primarily, other reforms have been made without the benefit of a referendum, for example the reform of financing political parties. Why should one reform be subject to referendum approval and not others? In a country with little tradition for referendums on issues other than those involving constitutional amendment, is it appropriate to begin such a process? How can we distinguish between legislative change that requires referendum approval and change that does not?

Secondly, referendums can oversell a reform, that is, the referendum process tends to present the proposed reform as "the best and the only" approach, whereas it is quite clear that improving Canadian democracy requires more than just electoral reform.

Third, referendums can be divisive. For relatively technical issues such as electoral system reform, it might be a better idea to put electoral reform at the center of electoral debates for a specific election, thereby creating opportunities for citizen dialogue and participation.

Finally, a careful analysis of the costs and benefits of holding a referendum should be done. If a referendum is deemed necessary, then the issue of "third-party" spending should be considered. The issue of "third-party" spending has been fought in the courts for well over a decade. Recently, the Ontario Court of Justice ruled that the section of the *Canada Elections Act* imposing restrictions on third parties during election campaigns "is an infringement of their constitutional right to political expression."[13] The Alberta Court of Appeal also recently dealt with the issue of third-party spending, ruling that there was insufficient evidence to determine whether money in Canadian political campaigns was "a pressing and substantial concern for fair elections in Canada." This case was recently appealed to the Supreme Court of Canada, where the decision was reserved at the time of writing this Report.[14] Although it applies to referendums relating to the *Constitution of Canada*, the *Referendum Act* could be amended to apply to the issue of electoral system reform.[15] The Act sets out rules for conducting referendums, including the registration of referendum committees, and imposes limits on referendum expenses. In general, the experience in other jurisdictions, particularly New Zealand's, has indicated that the issue of third-party advertising may justify imposing some limits.

Given the preceding discussion, the Commission makes the following recommendations.

Recommendation 19

The federal government should prepare draft legislation on a mixed member proportional electoral system as proposed in this Report. After drafting the legislation, a Parliamentary committee should initiate a public consultation process on the proposed new electoral system.

Recommendation 20

The public consultation process should be broadly representative and adequately resourced. It could consider the option of holding a referendum.

Recommendation 21

Elections Canada should be given at least a two-year preparation period before an election under the new electoral system is held.

6.2 Support for Democratic Participation After Electoral Reform

Electoral reform legislation should include a provision for formal review of the new system after a period of time, perhaps following two or three elections conducted under the new system. Such a review would examine how the new electoral system is functioning, and determine whether any improvements or modifications are necessary.

Recommendation 22

An ad hoc Parliamentary committee should review the new electoral system after three general elections have been conducted under the new electoral rules.

In addition, it is important to recognize the need for ongoing support for enhancing our democratic institutions and practices. Throughout the Commission's engagement process, citizens expressed a desire for more opportunities to reflect upon and raise questions about our system of governance. Recent research confirms this growing sentiment, suggesting that many Canadians would like to see the "reform of the country's political institutions at the top of the political agenda, making them more open and democratic."[16] In general, citizens no longer accept a passive, deferential role in the political system. Instead, they desire a real voice in the political decision-making processes, and more responsive, accountable, and effective political institutions. Increasingly, many Canadians are questioning various aspects of our democratic practices, including the role of Members of Parliament, the eligible age to vote, the possibility of Internet voting, and political party financing rules.

Of course, the concept of democracy and all that it entails can have many interpretations. In the Canadian context, however, belief in and support of "public participation, inclusiveness and responsiveness" are key aspects of our system of democratic governance: "…any contemporary definition of Canadian democracy must include public institutions and decision-making practices that are defined by public participation, that this participation must be inclusive of all Canadians, and that government outcomes must be responsive to the views of Canadians."[17] And although there are many institutions striving to improve aspects of our system of democracy (for example, improvements to our electoral rules, or to the operation of the House of Commons and the Senate) we need to continually examine our system of democracy and its performance in various contexts.

To that end, many provinces and the federal government have created departments specifically charged with reviewing democratic institutions or instituting reforms. For example, the democratic review processes in Quebec, New Brunswick, and Ontario explore opportunities to ensure that the system of governance is more relevant to its citizens (see, for further information, section 2.4). In addition, Prime Minister Paul Martin's recently introduced cabinet includes a minister responsible for democratic reform, who has been tasked with restoring trust in government. Among the commitments to democratic reform made by Prime Minister Martin are: "allowing more free votes in the House of Commons, giving Parliament a greater role in reviewing government appointments, allowing House Committees to influence and shape policy, and expanding the role of Parliamentary Secretaries so they can be a fundamental link between Ministers and Parliamentarians." He has also expressed an interest in strengthening ethical standards in the House of Commons.[18] All of these initiatives represent positive developments.

The responsibility for creating healthy democratic relationships and institutions should be shared by all levels of government and by citizens in general. Democracy is not a static process, but something that changes with society's needs and aspirations. It requires our constant tending. We cannot be complacent: there is a need for continued monitoring, consultation, research, and reform. Given that democracy is much more than just electoral system reform, the Commission makes the following recommendation.

Recommendation 23

A federal government department or agency should be made responsible for engaging in an ongoing dialogue with Canadians and citizens' groups on issues of democratic performance and change, and should be invited to reflect annually on the state of Canadian democracy, including representation issues relating to women, minority group members, Aboriginal people, and youth.

6.3 Conclusion

Chapter 6 explored options for initiating a process for reforming Canada's electoral system. Different models for engaging the public in discussion and debate about electoral system reform were presented, notably British Columbia's citizens' assembly, Quebec's Estates-General, and Prince Edward Island's Electoral Reform Commission. All of these approaches included citizen engagement as part of the decision-making process. Based on the Commission's own research and consultation, and drawing on the experiences of provincial initiatives, we recommended that the federal government draft legislation that would introduce a mixed member proportional electoral system, and include some form of citizen engagement process to review this proposed legislation.

We also noted that there is no constitutional requirement for a referendum to endorse changes to the electoral system. Finally, we recommended a mechanism for reviewing the new system, and for allowing the public to indicate its satisfaction or dissatisfaction with the reforms and with other aspects of democratic performance.

1   The Liberals won this massive majority with 58 percent of the popular vote in the 2001 provincial election. The New Democratic Party took a mere two seats with 22 percent of the vote, and the Green Party won no seats despite capturing just over 12 percent of the popular vote.

2   N. Ruff, "BC Deliberative Democracy: The Citizens' Assembly and Electoral Reform 2003–2005." Paper presented to the annual conference of the Canadian Political Science Association, 1 June 2003, Halifax at 7; cf. G. Gibson, *Report on the Constitution of the Citizens' Assembly on Electoral Reform*, 23 December 2002, Vancouver at 9–17.

3   In May 2003 the government nominated Jack Blaney, former president of Simon Fraser University, as chair of the Citizens' Assembly.

4   This 60/60 proposal was inserted into the Citizens' Assembly's terms of reference by the government; it was not part of Gordon Gibson's recommendations.

5   Québec, Ministre responsable de la Réforme des institutions démocratiques, 2002.

6   For further details, see, Electoral Reform Commission, online: <http://www.gov.pe.ca/electoralreform/index.php3> (date accessed: 19 December 2003).

7   See, Prince Edward Island Electoral Reform Commission, *Report*, 2003 at 100. Online: <http://www.gov.pe.ca/electoralreform/index.php3> (date accessed: 6 January 2004).

8   Turnout in this first referendum, however, was quite low—only 55 percent of registered voters. Mixed member proportional was the choice of just over 70 percent of these voters as the best alternative model. Single transferable vote received support from 18 percent, and AV from 7 percent. P. Harris, "New Zealand Adopts PR: A Research Director's View" (2001) 22:6 *Policy Options* at 33–34.

9   *Ibid.* at 34.

10 M. Mendelsohn, A. Parkin and A. Van Kralingen, "Getting from Here to There: A Process for Electoral Reform in Canada" (2001) 22:6 *Policy Options* at 55–56.

11 R. Katz, "Reforming the Italian Electoral Law, 1993," M.S. Shugart and M.P. Wattenberg, eds., *Mixed Member Electoral Systems: The Best of Both Worlds?* (Oxford University Press 2001) at 96–98.

12 M. Mendelsohn, A. Parkin and A. Van Kralingen, *supra* note 10 at 57.

13 G. Abbate, "Election spending rule quashed" (16 October 2003) *The Globe and Mail* at A15. See, *Canada (Elections Canada) v. National Citizen's Coalition*, [2003] (O.J.) No.3939 (O.C.J.).

14 See, *Harper v. Canada (Attorney General)* [2002] (A.J.) No. 1542 (A.B.C.A.). The Supreme Court of Canada decision regarding *The Attorney General of Canada v. Stephen Joseph Harper* (29618) was reserved at the time of the writing of this Report.

15 *Referendum Act*, R.S.C. 1992, c. 30.

16 See, for example, Centre for Research and Information on Canada (CRIC) (28 October 2003) *Portraits of Canada*, online: <http://www.cric.ca/en_re/portraits/index.html> (date accessed: 19 December 2003). In the CRIC survey, 48% of Canadians identified democratic reform as a priority for government.

17 Centre for Canadian Studies, Mount Allison University, *Canadian Democratic Audit: An Overview*, online: <http://www.mta.ca/faculty/arts-letters/canadian_studies/demaudit_overview_15aug.pdf> (date accessed: 5 January 2004).

18 Paul Martin Times, online: <www.paulmartin.ca> "Martin Announces Detailed Plan for New Government," 12 December 2003 (date accessed: 19 December 2003).

Conclusion Reforming Electoral Democracy in Canada

> "Simply reforming the voting system will not give Canadians full control over their democracy. Partisanship will still affect Senate appointments, the Prime Minister will still be able to set the date for an election, and the Head of State will still not be a Canadian chosen by the population at large. Grouping everything together offers the advantage of putting inevitable constitutional changes on the table once. We should not fear these changes; they will allow citizens to take their country's political destiny fully in hand." [Translation]
>
> Gabriel Racle, Ottawa. Feedback from the Law Commission of Canada's consultation process. (Received: 30 December 2002.)

Canada inherited its first-past-the-post electoral system from Great Britain over 200 years ago, at a time when significant sections of the Canadian population, including women, Aboriginal people, and non-property owners, were disenfranchised. Throughout the first half of the 19th century and for 50 years after Confederation, the strengths of our electoral system were evident: it fostered competition between two major parties and provided the successful party with a strong, albeit artificial, legislative majority—at a time when party discipline and cohesiveness were less powerful forces than they are today. Territory, embodied in the direct link between the Member of Parliament and his (for they were all men) constituents, was the most important aspect of a citizen's political identity and the pre-eminent feature of prevailing notions of representation.[1]

The socioeconomic underpinnings of this system of representation began to erode in the aftermath of the First World War, under the impact of western immigration, urbanization and industrialization. New classes and groups—farmers, workers, and women—sought entry into the political system, and mobilized within new political parties whose capacity for growth was restricted by an electoral formula that systematically favoured the two major parties. It was during this period that the first, short-lived experiments with alternative electoral systems were attempted, mostly in the newly settled western provinces.

In the 1970s and 1980s, further social and political change, including the rise of new social movements espousing a different kind of political discourse, placed additional strain on our electoral and party systems. New voices representing women, Aboriginal peoples, the environmental movement, newcomers to Canada, and youth began to struggle for entry into what they saw as the closed world of traditional politics. The idea of moving toward a system with an element of proportional representation emerged to compensate for the distortions of our first-past-the-post system.

In the past decade or so, a number of established democracies—New Zealand, Japan, Italy, and the United Kingdom[2]—have either engaged in significant electoral reform or encouraged a wide public debate about the topic. Electoral system engineers have also designed new models in many of the new states that have emerged out of the collapse of the Soviet Union. The vast majority of these new systems have been mixed, incorporating the "best of both worlds," namely the accountability and geographic representation that is one of the strengths of first-past-the-post systems and other plurality formulas, along with the demographic representativeness and fairness of proportional representation systems.

At the same time, across Canada there are signs that a growing number of Canadians are no longer satisfied with our current electoral system. It is becoming increasingly apparent that the current electoral system no longer responds to 21st century Canadian democratic values. This is evidenced by the various electoral reform review initiatives in British Columbia, Quebec, New Brunswick, and Prince Edward Island; the research, education campaigns, and electoral reform lobbying conducted by civil society groups; and polling data that reveals decreased support for the existing electoral system. Many Canadians desire an electoral system that better reflects the society in which they live—one that includes a broader diversity of ideas and is more representative of Canadian society.

For these reasons, the Commission recommends adding an element of proportionality to our electoral system. We believe that some element of proportionality would allow Parliament to more completely represent our society and to lower the barriers to greater diversity among our representatives. An element of proportionality would also reduce the regional imbalances in the legislative caucuses of all the major parties in Canada. It would promote fairness, and encourage the entry of new voices in the legislature, which would in turn invigorate this country's parliamentary democracy. And, finally, it has the potential to revitalize voter turnout.

There would be adjustments and implications to adopting a mixed member proportional electoral system. For example, coalition or minority governments would occur more frequently. However, as demonstrated in Chapter 5, this consequence of electoral reform does not represent a radical departure from the status quo. In fact, judging by international experience, coalition governments can be even more effective in formulating coherent economic policy than those formed in majority–plurality systems.

Because of the many potential benefits to reforming the current electoral system, it should be a priority item on the political agenda. While electoral reform is not a panacea for all of the country's political problems, nor will it single handedly invigorate our democracy, it is a necessary and vital step in improving democracy in Canada. Without it, we are faced with trying to make a 19th century institution work within a 21st century society. For a growing number of Canadians, this is no longer acceptable. This Report is designed to inform and invigorate a movement toward electoral reform that can enhance Canadian democracy.

---

1 T. Knight, "Unconstitutional Democracy? A Charter Challenge to Canada's Electoral System" (1999) 57:1 *University of Toronto Faculty Law Review* at 33.

2 Electoral reform has take place in the United Kingdom with the creation of regional parliaments in Scotland and Wales, both of which have adopted a mixed member proportional electoral system. The United Kingdom itself has also gone further down the road toward electoral reform than Canada, with its creation of the Independent Commission on the Voting System (the Jenkins Commission).

Recommendations

Adding an Element of Proportionality to the Electoral System

Recommendation 1
The Law Commission of Canada recommends adding an element of proportionality to Canada's electoral system.

Recommendation 2
The Law Commission of Canada recommends that Canada adopt a mixed member proportional electoral system.

Recommendation 3
A mixed member proportional system should be based on giving voters TWO votes: one for a constituency representative and one for a party list. The party vote should determine who is to be elected from provincial and territorial lists as drawn up by the parties before the election.

Recommendation 4
Two-thirds of the members of the House of Commons should be elected in constituency races using the first-past-the-post method, and the remaining one-third should be elected from provincial or territorial party lists. In addition, one list seat each should be allotted to Nunavut, Northwest Territories, and Yukon.

Recommendation 5
Within the context of a mixed member proportional system, Parliament should adopt a *flexible* list system that provides voters with the option of either endorsing the party "slate" or "ticket," or of indicating a preference for a candidate within the list.

Promoting Women's Representation

Recommendation 6

Parliament should require political parties to develop initiatives and policies to promote equal representation of women in the House of Commons. Parties should be instructed to consider a range of issues, including:

- parity on party lists,

- the use of quotas for party lists and constituency nominations,

- recruiting policies for women candidates,

- incentive measures for women to participate in politics,

- support for campaign financing, including measures to enhance access to candidacy, and

- the inclusion of more women in cabinet, if a party is elected as the government.

Following the first general election under the new electoral system, political parties should also be required to submit reports to Parliament outlining how they addressed these issues.

Recommendation 7

A Parliamentary committee should subsequently review the parties' reports on the measures they have taken to promote the equal representation of women in the House of Commons.

Promoting Minority Group Representation

Recommendation 8

Parliament should require political parties to develop initiatives and policies to promote greater representation of minority group members in the House of Commons. Parties should be instructed to consider a range of issues, including:

- minority group candidates on party lists,

- the use of quotas for party lists and constituency nominations,

- recruiting policies for minority group candidates,

- incentive measures for minority group candidates to participate in politics,

- support for campaign financing, including measures to enhance access to candidacy, and

- the inclusion of more minority group members in cabinet, if a party is elected as the government.

Following the first general election under the new electoral system, political parties should also be required to submit reports to Parliament outlining how they addressed these issues.

Recommendation 9
A Parliamentary committee should subsequently review the parties' reports on the measures they have taken to promote greater representation of minority group members in the House of Commons.

Promoting Youth Representation

Recommendation 10
Parliament should require that political parties examine options for increasing youth participation and representation in mainstream political decision making. This process should be based on broad and inclusive consultations, and should consider ways to better reflect the perspectives of youth in the system of democratic governance. Political parties should also be required to submit reports to Parliament outlining the measures they have taken to promote youth participation and representation. A Parliamentary committee should subsequently review the parties' reports.

Promoting Aboriginal Representation

Recommendation 11

Parliament should require political parties, in consultation with First Nations, Métis and Inuit peoples, to develop initiatives and policies to promote greater representation of Aboriginal people in the House of Commons. Parties should be instructed to consider a range of issues, including:

- Aboriginal candidates on party lists,

- the use of quotas for party lists and constituency nominations,

- recruiting policies for Aboriginal candidates,

- incentive measures for Aboriginal peoples to participate in politics,

- support for campaign financing, including measures to enhance access to candidacy, and

- the inclusion of Aboriginal people in cabinet, if a party is elected as the government.

Following the first general election under the new electoral system, political parties should also be required to submit reports to Parliament outlining how they addressed these issues. A Parliamentary committee should subsequently review the parties' reports on the measures they have taken to promote greater representation of Aboriginal people in the House of Commons.

Recommendation 12

The federal government, in consultation with First Nations, Métis, and Inuit peoples, should explore the possibility of introducing Aboriginal Electoral Districts, as recommended by the Royal Commission on Electoral Reform and Party Financing, or a "House of Aboriginal Peoples," consistent with the recommendations of the Royal Commission on Aboriginal Peoples.

Electoral System Design Issues

Recommendation 13

There should be no legal threshold for gaining access to the list (compensatory) seats.

Recommendation 14

A party should be eligible for compensatory provincial list seats only if it presents candidates for election in at least one-third of the constituencies in the relevant province. In Prince Edward Island, any party wishing to be eligible for the list seats would have to contest the single-member constituency seat in that province. In Nunavut, Northwest Territories, and Yukon, any party wishing to be eligible for a list seat would have to contest the single-member constituency seat in the relevant territory.

Recommendation 15

There should be no legal restrictions on *double inclusion*. That is, candidates should be able to run both in a constituency and on the party list at the provincial or territorial level.

Recommendation 16

Provincial and territorial list Members of Parliament should have all the rights and privileges of constituency Members of Parliament.

Recommendation 17

Parties represented in the House of Commons should develop protocols for ensuring the effective co-functioning of constituency and list Members of Parliament, including consideration of methods for informing constituency Members of Parliament of issues or cases being taken up by list Members of Parliament.

Recommendation 18

Vacancies in the directly-elected (constituency) portion of Members of Parliament should be filled by means of a by-election, while vacancies among list Members of Parliament should be filled by the candidate who was ranked next highest on the party list for the province or territory in question.

Implementation

Recommendation 19

The federal government should prepare draft legislation on a mixed member proportional electoral system as proposed in this Report. After drafting the legislation, a Parliamentary committee should initiate a public consultation process on the proposed new electoral system.

Recommendation 20

The public consultation process should be broadly representative and adequately resourced. It could consider the option of holding a referendum.

Recommendation 21

Elections Canada should be given at least a two-year preparation period before an election under the new electoral system is held.

Monitoring / Review Process

Recommendation 22

An ad hoc Parliamentary committee should review the new electoral system after three general elections have been conducted under the new electoral rules.

Recommendation 23

A federal government department or agency should be made responsible for engaging in an ongoing dialogue with Canadians and citizens' groups on issues of democratic performance and change, and should be invited to reflect annually on the state of Canadian democracy, including representation issues relating to women, minority group members, Aboriginal people, and youth.

Appendix A: Creation of Regions within Quebec and Ontario for a Mixed Member Proportional Electoral System

Please note that the population figures below are taken from the Chief Electoral Officer's report on the General Election of 2000, and reflect 1996 census data.

QUEBEC

Region 1—North and East Quebec, outside Montreal

Riding name	Population
Abitibi–Baie–James–Nunavik	95,948
Bas-Richelieu–Nicolet–Bécancour	87,597
Beauce	99,453
Beauport–Montmorency–Côte-de-Beaupré–Île-d'Orléans	101,444
Bellechasse–Etchemins–Montmagny–L'Islet	83,911
Berthier–Montcalm	125,619
Bonaventure–Gaspé–Îles-de-la-Madeleine–Pabok	75,543
Brome–Missisquoi	84,359
Champlain	88,944
Charlesbourg–Jacques–Cartier	105,007
Charlevoix	78,659
Chicoutimi–Le Fjord	86,252
Compton–Stanstead	77,974
Drummond	84,250
Frontenac–Mégantic	69,701
Gatineau	120,369
Hull–Aylmer	97,240
Joliette	95,470
Jonquière	68,715

Kamouraska–Rivière-du-Loup–Témiscouata–Les-Basques	88,621
Lac-Saint-Jean–Saguenay	69,777
Laurentides	124,766
Lévis-et-Chutes-de-la-Chaudière	122,255
Lotbinière–L'Érable	69,952
Louis–Hébert	98,496
Manicouagan	55,018
Matapédia–Matane	74,237
Pontiac–Gatineau–Labelle	103,404
Portneuf	89,315
Québec	99,661
Québec-Est	109,210
Richmond–Athabaska	98,830
Rimouski–Neigette-et-la Mitis	72,837
Roberval	73,139
Saint-Hyacinthe–Bagot	94,057
Saint-Maurice	79,230
Shefford	93,311
Sherbrooke	97,084
Témiscamingue	85,163
Trois-Rivières	92,989
Total:	**3,617,807**

Region 1 has 40 ridings, 23 won by the Bloc Québécois (BQ), 16 by the Liberal Party (LIB) and 1 by the Progressive Conservative Party (PC) in the 2000 federal election. If these figures are reduced by one-third following the Scottish Model, then the region has 27 ridings, 15 of them won by the BQ, 11 by the LIB, and 1 by the PC. This region would receive 13 additional list seats.

Region 2—Montreal and Immediate Vicinity

Riding Name	Population
Ahuntsic	104,960
Anjou–Rivière-des-Prairies	95,099
Argenteuil–Papineau–Mirabel	101,268

Beauharnois–Salaberry	93,685
Bourassa	90,902
Brossard–La Prairie	98,516
Chambly	102,009
Châteauguay	110,605
Hochelaga–Maisonneuve	93,160
Lac-Saint-Louis	106,473
Lasalle–Émard	97,542
Laurier–Sainte-Marie	96,640
Laval-Centre	106,931
Laval-Est	106,942
Laval-Ouest	116,520
Longueuil	83,442
Mercier	95,070
Mont-Royal	95,616
Notre-Dame-de-Grâce–Lachine	100,927
Outremont	95,665
Papineau–Saint-Denis	105,607
Pierrefonds–Dollard	110,147
Repentigny	120,562
Rivière-des-Mille-Îsles	112,800
Rosemont–Petite-Patrie	102,375
Saint-Bruno–Saint-Hubert	100,756
Saint-Jean	92,132
Saint-Lambert	87,895
Saint-Laurent–Cartierville	96,788
Saint-Léonard–Saint-Michel	103,336
Terrebonne–Blainville	112,750
Vaudreuil–Soulanges	95,318
Verchères–Les Partriotes	103,001
Verdun–Saint-Henri–Saint-Paul–Pointe Saint-Charles	91,481
Westmount–Ville-Marie	94,058
PARTY TOTALS:	**3,520,978**

Region 2 has 35 ridings, 20 won by the LIB and 15 by the BQ in 2000. Reducing these totals by one-third results in: 23 ridings,

13 won by the LIB and 10 by the BQ. This region would receive 12 additional list seats.

ONTARIO

Region 1—North and East Ontario

Riding Name	Population
Algoma–Manitoulin	75,120
Barrie–Simcoe–Bradford	124,450
Durham	106,045
Glengarry–Prescott–Russell	100,204
Haliburton–Victoria–Brock	108,011
Hastings–Frontenac–Lennox and Addington	97,025
Kenora–Rainy River	79,550
Kingston and the Islands	111,411
Lanark–Carleton	124,295
Leeds–Grenville	96,284
Markham	119,462
Nepean–Carleton	111,886
Nickel Belt	82,576
Nipissing	76,047
Northumberland	98,971
Oshawa	107,771
Ottawa Centre	109,903
Ottawa–Orleans	100,659
Ottawa South	111,532
Ottawa–Vanier	103,418
Ottawa West–Nepean	108,564
Parry Sound–Muskoka	82,853
Peterborough	109,902
Pickering–Ajax–Uxbridge	119,171
Prince Edward–Hastings	93,743
Renfrew–Nipissing–Pembroke	97,571
Sault Ste. Marie	80,054
Simcoe North	106,630
Stormont–Dundas–Charlottenburgh	95,834

Sudbury	86,243
Thunder Bay–Atikokan	78,360
Thunder Bay–Superior North	79,680
Timiskaming–Cochrane	75,769
Timmins–James Bay	79,627
Whitby–Ajax	113,924
York North	117,859
TOTALS:	**3,570,404**

Region 1 has 36 ridings, 34 won by the LIB and 2 by the Canadian Alliance Party (CA) in 2000. Reducing these totals by one-third results in: 24 risings, 23 won by the LIB and 1 by the CA. This region would receive 11 additional list seats.

Region 2—South and West Ontario

Riding Name	Population
Ancaster–Dundas–Flamborough–Aldershot	95,568
Brant	105,679
Bruce–Grey–Owen Sound	98,317
Burlington	99,763
Cambridge	115,848
Chatham–Kent Essex	105,174
Dufferin–Peel–Wellington–Grey	110,571
Elgin–Middlesex–London	101,573
Erie–Lincoln	94,672
Essex	110,713
Guelph–Wellington	110,836
Haldimond–Norfolk–Brant	98,989
Halton	119,537
Hamilton East	97,491
Hamilton Mountain	105,316
Hamilton West	100,149
Huron–Bruce	95,981
Kitchener Centre	109,398
Kitchener–Waterloo	114,390
Lambton–Kent–Middlesex	98,542

London–Fanshawe	103,511
London North Centre	104,291
London West	106,531
Niagara Centre	102,510
Niagara Falls	93,103
Oakville	105,572
Oxford	97,142
Perth–Middlesex	94,576
Sarnia–Lambton	90,697
Simcoe–Grey	111,559
St. Catherines	106,105
Stoney Creek	103,863
Waterloo–Wellington	107,797
Windsor–St.Clair	106,108
Windsor West	108,119
TOTAL:	**3,629,991**

Region 2 has 35 ridings, 34 won by the LIB and 1 by the New Democratic Party (NDP) in 2000. Reducing these totals by one-third results in: 23 ridings, 22 won by the LIB and 1 by the NDP. This region would receive 12 additional list seats.

Region 3—Toronto and Vicinity

Riding Name	Population
Beaches–East York	108,997
Bramalea–Gore–Malton–Springdale	120,699
Brampton Centre	106,393
Brampton West–Mississauga	133,554
Davenport	103,074
Don Valley East	113,338
Don Valley West	108,254
Eglington–Lawrence	108,410
Etobicoke Centre	104,398
Etobicoke–Lakeshore	109,253
Etobicoke North	115,067
Mississauga Centre	114,855

Mississauga East	108,843
Mississauga South	100,260
Mississauga West	128,029
Oak Ridges	129,379
Parkdale–High Park	105,740
Scarborough–Agincourt	107,030
Scarborough Centre	114,844
Scarborough East	108,644
Scarborough–Rouge River	120,264
Scarborough–Southwest	108,178
St. Paul's	103,725
Thornhill	106,628
Toronto Centre–Rosedale	114,416
Toronto Danforth	100,678
Trinity–Spadina	101,104
Vaughn–King–Aurora	119,117
Willowdale	107,416
York Centre	107,370
York South–Weston	110,264
York West	104,957
TOTAL:	**3,553,178**

Region 3 has 32 ridings, all of them won by the LIB in 2000. Reducing these totals by one-third results in 22 seats, all of them won by the LIB. This region would receive 11 additional list seats.

Appendix B: Public Consultation and Engagement Strategy

The Law Commission of Canada employed a multifaceted public consultation and engagement strategy to gather the insights and opinions of a broad cross section of Canadians on electoral system reform. In addition to conducting research and producing a discussion paper, the Commission held a study panel, took part in academic conferences, hosted a series of public consultations in different parts of the country, helped organize and co-sponsor special events and forums dealing with democratic and electoral reform, met with concerned citizens and groups, and launched a consultation questionnaire on the Commission's website.

Research

The following research papers were commissioned by or prepared for the Commission as part of its electoral reform project:

- Archer, K., *A Question of Values: Representation in Canada's Contemporary System of Governance* (Ottawa: Law Commission of Canada, 2003).

- Crocker, R., *Renewing Canadian Democracy: Citizen Engagement in Voting System Reform – Phase Two: Forum,* Ottawa, 25–26 April, 2002, Report on Proceedings (Ottawa: Law Commission of Canada, 2002).

- Earles, K. and Findlay T., *Rethinking Representation: Toward Democratic Governance in Canada* (Ottawa: Law Commission of Canada, 2003).

- Gordon, L., *Renewing Canadian Democracy: Citizen Engagement in Voting System Reform – Phase 3: A plan for 21st century democratic renewal in Canada* (Ottawa: Law Commission of Canada, 2002).

- Mallet, M., *Votes, Victories and Values: Probing the Issue of Electoral Reform in Canada* (A summary of the Commission's background paper on electoral reform) (Ottawa: Law Commission of Canada, 2001).

- Pilon, D., *Renewing Canadian Democracy: Citizen Engagement in Voting System Reform – Phase One: Lessons from Around the World* (Ottawa: Law Commission of Canada, 2002).

- Schmidt, J., *Aboriginal Representation in Government: A Comparative Examination* (Ottawa: Law Commission of Canada, 2003).

- Schwartz, B. and Rettie D., *Valuing Canadians: The options for voting system reform in Canada* (Ottawa: Law Commission of Canada, 2003).

- Seidle, F.L., *Electoral System Reform in Canada: Objectives, Advocacy and Implications for Governance* (Ottawa: Canadian Policy Research Networks, Inc., 2002).

- Tremblay, M., *Political Representation in Canada: Theoretical and Empirical Considerations* (Ottawa: Law Commission of Canada, 2003).

Discussion Paper

In October 2002, the Commission released *Renewing Democracy: Debating Electoral Reform in Canada*, a discussion paper on electoral system reform. *Renewing Democracy* examined various aspects of the electoral reform debate, asking fundamental questions about the current voting system. What values should be reflected in our voting system? Does the current system adequately reflect these values? Are there ways to remedy concerns with the current voting system without switching to a different method of voting? If not, should we consider an alternative voting system?

The Commission invited Canadians to send their comments and feedback on the issues and questions raised throughout *Renewing Democracy*. In response, the Commission received e-mails, letters, and phone calls from a cross section of Canadian electoral reform organizations, current and former politicians, union representatives, women's groups, political scientists, media, and various non-governmental organizations, among others. In addition, *Renewing Democracy* was assigned reading and discussion material in several university-level political studies courses.

Public Consultations

To help stimulate discussion and debate about electoral system reform, the Commission, in partnership with non-governmental organizations and community groups, organized a series of public consultations across the country. At each session, the Commission presented its Discussion Paper, followed by comments from a discussant, and a moderated question and discussion period. The sessions were held in these locations.

- **Toronto—November 12, 2002**
  Auditorium of the Metro-Central YMCA,
  20 Grosvenor Street
  This consultation was attended by more than 100 people, and was moderated by Mr. Patrick Boyer, QC, Adjunct Professor, Department of Political Science, University of Guelph. The discussant was Professor Ed Morgan, University of Toronto.

- **Ottawa—November 19, 2002**
  Government Conference Centre, Sussex Room,
  2 Rideau Street
  This consultation was co-sponsored by the Canadian Study of Parliament Group and was attended by more than 50 people. The moderator was Professor Christopher Waddell, School of Journalism and Communication, Carleton University, and the discussant was Professor Jennifer Smith, Department of Political Science, Dalhousie University.

- **Vancouver—November 21, 2002**
  Vancouver Public Library, Alice MacKay Room
  350 West Georgia Street
  This consultation was attended by approximately 30 people, and was moderated by Professor Richard Johnston, Department of Political Science, University of British Columbia. The discussant was Professor Andrew Petter, Dean of Law, University of Victoria.

- **Charlottetown—December 4, 2002**
University of Prince Edward Island, Duffy Amphitheatre
This consultation was co-sponsored by the Institute of Island Studies and was attended by approximately 60 people. The moderator was Mr. Alan Buchanan, and the discussant was Mr. Wade MacLauchlan, President, University of Prince Edward Island.

- **Montreal—January 14, 2003**
Moot Court, Faculty of Law, McGill University
3644 Peel Street
This consultation was co-sponsored by the Institute for Research on Public Policy (IRPP) and was attended by approximately 40 people. The moderator was Professor Roderick Macdonald, Faculty of Law, McGill University and the discussant was Mr. Hugh Segal, President, IRPP.

- **London—February 4, 2003**
Stevenson-Hunt Room, London Public Library
251 Dundas Street
This consultation was co-sponsored by the London Chapter of the Council of Canadians and was attended by approximately 80 people. The moderator was Professor Grant Huscroft, Faculty of Law, University of Western Ontario, and the discussant was Professor Paul Nesbitt-Larking, Department of Political Science, Huron University College.

- **Calgary—April 30, 2003**
John Dutton Theatre, 2nd Floor, WR Castell Library
616 MacLeod Trail S.E.
This consultation was co-sponsored by Canada West Foundation and the Sheldon M. Chumir Foundation for Ethics in Leadership and was attended by approximately 40 people. The moderator was Dr. Marsha Hanen, President, Sheldon M. Chumir Foundation for Ethics in Leadership, and the discussant was Dr. Roger Gibbins, President and CEO, Canada West Foundation.

- **Edmonton—May 5, 2003**
  Room 237, University of Alberta Law Centre,
  University of Alberta
  This consultation was co-sponsored by the Centre for
  Constitutional Studies and was attended by approximately
  45 people. The moderator was Dr. Tsvi Khana, Executive
  Director, Centre for Constitutional Studies, and the discussant
  was Professor David Smith, Department of Political Science,
  University of Saskatchewan.

Special Events and Forums

The Commission organized and/or co-sponsored a series of special
events and forums aimed at encouraging Canadians to discuss and
debate various aspects of electoral reform.

- **Targeted Constituencies Forum—Renewing Democracy:
  Citizen Engagement in Voting System Reform—
  April 25–26, 2002**
  Government Conference Centre, 2 Rideau Street, Ottawa
  The goal of this event was to bring together a diverse group
  of academics, provincial representatives, citizens interested in
  democratic participation and members of under-represented
  communities of interest to examine methods for engaging
  Canadians on issues associated with the electoral system and
  its reform. This event was attended by more than 50 people.

- **De la parole aux actes : regard de femme sur la
  démocratie—January 24–25, 2003.**
  Marché Bonsesours (Métro Champs-de-Mars), Montréal
  This colloquium was organized by the Collectif : féminisme
  et démocratie and co-sponsored by the Law Commission
  of Canada.

- **Roundtable on Women and Politics—March 22–23, 2003.**
  Centre Block, Parliament Hill
  This roundtable was organized by the National Association of
  Women and the Law, and co-sponsored by the Law Commission
  of Canada.

- **Voter Apathy: Is the System Broke?—May 21, 2003**
  UBC Robson Square, Vancouver
  This event was organized by the Canadian Unity Council, the Centre for Research and Information on Canada, and Continuing Studies at the University of British Columbia, and co-sponsored by the Vancouver Sun and the Law Commission of Canada.

- **Canadian Association of Former Parliamentarians— June 2, 2003**
  Room 200, West Block, Parliament Hill
  In March 2003, the Commission administered a questionnaire on electoral system reform to all members of the Canadian Association of Former Parliamentarians. Bernard Colas, Commissioner, presented the results of this questionnaire at the Association's annual meeting.

- **Ready, Set, Vote!—September 30, 2003**
  Metro Hall, 55 John Street, Toronto
  This event was presented by YouCAN! in partnership with the Law Commission of Canada, Toronto Youth Cabinet, City of Toronto and Elections Canada. More than 200 youth from area high schools discussed and debated various issues relating to Canada's system of democratic governance.

- **Forum—Women's Representation in the House of Commons: vox populix–October 31, 2003.**
  University of Ottawa, Room 140, New Residence Building
  The forum was co-sponsored by the University of Ottawa Centre for Research on Women and Politics and the Law Commission of Canada. Approximately 100 people attended to discuss issues relating to women's representation in the House of Commons. In addition to presentations by academics, and current and former women politicians, participants were given an opportunity to ask questions and debate issues.

Study Panel

On 25 October 2001, the Commission organized a Study Panel on electoral system reform. The purpose of the Study Panel was to provide advice and guidance to the Commission regarding the electoral reform project, to help ensure that the Commission's work reflected the interests of all Canadians and that we were engaged in innovative and multi-disciplinary research that accommodates a diversity of perspectives. The Study Panel was attended by 18 people drawn from a broad cross section of Canadians, including academics, government officials, non-governmental representatives, and experts on electoral system reform. Following the study panel, participants took part in an online discussion group to further explore some of the questions and issues relating to electoral system reform.

Conferences

The Commission delivered presentations, moderated panels, and attended several conferences throughout the course of the electoral reform project.

- **The Democratic Reform Project: Federalism and Legislatures Conference—April 4–7, 2002**
  Kempenfelt Bay Conference Centre, Innisfil, Ontario

- **Congress of the Social Sciences and Humanities: Breakfast on Campus with Rex Murphy—April 25, 2002**
  The Commission organized a presentation on "Renewing Democracy."

- **Canadian Association of Law Teachers—May 25, 2002**
  The Commission organized a session on electoral system reform.

- **Atlantic Provinces Political Science Association Conference—October 6, 2002**
  St. Thomas University, Fredericton

- **Constitution and Democracy: Ten Years After the Charlottetown Accord (Association of Canadian Studies Conference)—October 26, 2003.**
  Montreal

- **Roundtable—The Reform of Democratic Institutions (Institute for Research on Public Policy)—March 4, 2003**
  Royal Ontario Museum, Toronto

- **Squaring the Circle: The Place of Courts in a Democratic Canada—March 15, 2003**
  Mount Allison University, Department of Canadian Studies, Sackville, New Brunswick

- **Canadian Association of Political Science (Session on Electoral Reform)—June 1, 2003**
  Dalhousie University, Halifax

- **Roundtable–The Reform of Democratic Institutions II (Institute for Research on Public Policy)– September 10, 2003**
  Montreal

Meetings and Presentations

During the electoral reform project, the Commission met with more than 30 different individuals and groups. Below are examples of some of these meetings and presentations.

- **Mount Allison University—March 13, 2002**
  Mount Allison University, Owens Art Gallery, Sackville, New Brunswick
  (Presentation to students)

- **Sackville Rotary Club—March 13, 2002**
  Mount Allison University, Owens Art Gallery, Sackville, New Brunswick
  (Presentation to Rotary Club Members)

- **Churchill Society for the Advancement of Parliamentary Democracy—April 4, 2003**
  Toronto
  (Presentation to Members)

- **Fair Vote Canada, Annual General Meeting—
  April 26, 2003**
  (Presentations to Fair Vote Canada—the Commission also
  attended the 2001 and 2002 annual meetings.)
  Ottawa

- **CCMD Armchair Discussion—Renewing Democracy:
  Debating Electoral Reform in Canada–October 30, 2003**
  Canadian Centre for Management Development, Ottawa

- **Mount Allison University: Academic Conference on
  Legislative Democracy—February 5 and 6, 2003**
  Sackville, New Brunswick

Internet Consultation Questionnaire

The Commission posted a questionnaire about electoral system
reform on its website. The questionnaire asked citizens their opinions
on a variety of questions relating to electoral system reform. For
example: Why do people feel alienated from their system of government? Do our political institutions reflect contemporary Canadian
values? How can we reduce the gap between governments and
citizens? Why is voting important? Why might young people choose
to not participate in the electoral process? Does our voting system
need to be changed? What values do we want to see reflected in our
electoral system? Does the current voting system adequately reflect
these values? If not, do we need to consider an alternative system that
might better reflect these values?

   The Commission's website also included a quiz on electoral system
reform, a discussion kit for those interested in holding their own
discussion group on electoral reform, and contact information for
providing the Commission with comments and feedback on its work.

Appendix C: Bibliography

Abbate, G., "Election spending rule quashed" *The Globe and Mail,* 16 October 2003 A15.

Aimer, P., "From Westminster Plurality to Continental Proportionality: Electoral System Change in New Zealand" in Henry Milner, ed., *Making Every Vote Count: Reassessing Canada's Electoral System* (Peterborough: Broadview Press, 1999) 145.

Archer, K. *A Question of Values: Representation in Canada's Contemporary System of Governance* (Ottawa: Law Commission of Canada, 2003).

Arseneau, T., "The Representation of Women and Aboriginals Under PR: Lessons from New Zealand" (November 1997) *Policy Options* 9.

Arseneau, T., "Electing Representative Legislatures: Lessons from New Zealand" in Henry Milner, ed., *Making Every Vote Count: Reassessing Canada's Electoral System* (Peterborough: Broadview Press, 1999) 133.

Aucoin, P. and Smith, J., "Proportional Representation: Misrepresenting Equality" (November 1997) *Policy Options* 30.

Barker, F., Boston, J., Levine, S., McLeay, E., and Roberts, N.S., "An Initial Assessment of the Consequences of MMP in New Zealand" in M. S. Shugart and M. P. Wattenberg, eds., *Mixed Member Electoral Systems: The Best of Both Worlds?.* (Oxford: Oxford University Press, 2001) 297.

Blais, A., "Criteria for Assessing Electoral Systems" (1999) 1:1 *Electoral Insight* 3.

Blais, A., Massicotte, L., and Dobrzynska, A., "Why is Turnout Higher in Some Countries than in Others?" (paper presented to the Symposium on Electoral Participation in Canada, Carleton University, Ottawa, Ontario, 18 February 2003), online: <http://www.elections.ca/loi/tur/tuh/Turnout Higher.pdf> (date accessed: 19 December 2003).

Boston, J., Levine, S., McLeay, E., Roberts, N.S., and Schmidt, H., "The Impact of Electoral Reform on the Public Service: The New Zealand Case" (1998) 57:3 *Australian Journal of Public Administration* 64.

Brams, S.J., and Fishburn, P.C., "Some Logical Defects of the Single Transferable Vote" in A. Lijphart and B. Grofman, eds., *Choosing an Electoral System: Issues and Alternatives* (New York: Praeger, 1984) 147.

Bricker, D., and Redfern, M., "Canadian Perspectives on the Voting System" (2001) 22:6 *Policy Options* 22.

Butler, D., "Electoral Systems" in D. Butler, H.R. Penniman and A. Ranney, eds., *Democracy at the Polls: A Comparative Study of Competitive National Elections* (Washington: American Enterprise Institute, 1981) 7.

Cairns, A., "The Electoral System and the Party System in Canada, 1921–1965" in O. Kruhlak, R. Schultz and S. Pobihushchy, eds., *The Canadian Political Process*, rev. ed., (Toronto: Holt, Rinehart and Winston, 1973) 133.

Canada, *A History of the Vote in Canada* (Ottawa–Public Works and Government Services Canada, 1997).

Canada, Committee for Aboriginal Electoral Reform, *The Path to Electoral Equality* (Ottawa, 1989).

Canada (Elections Canada) v. National Citizen's Coalition, [2003] (O.J.) No. 3939 (O.C.J.).

Canada, *Report of the Royal Commission on Aboriginal Peoples: Restructuring the Relationship*, vol. 2 (Ottawa: Supply and Services Canada, 1996).

Canada, Royal Commission on the Economic Union and Development Prospects for Canada, *Report: Volume Three* (Ottawa: Minister of Supply and Services, 1985).

Canada, Royal Commission on Electoral Reform and Party Financing, *Final Report Vol. I: Reforming Electoral Democracy* (Ottawa: Minister of Supply and Services, 1991).

Canada, Royal Commission on Electoral Reform and Party Financing, *Final Report Vol. 4: What Canadians Told Us* (Ottawa: Minister of Supply and Services, 1991).

Canada, Task Force on Canadian Unity, *A Future Together: Observations and Recommendations* (Canada: Minister of Supply and Services, 1979) (Chairmen: Jean-Luc Pepin and John P. Robarts).

Centre for Canadian Studies at Mount Allison University, *The Canada Democratic Audit*, online: <http://www.mta.ca/faculty/arts-letters /canadian_studies/audit.htm> (date accessed: 30 November 2003).

Centre for Research and Information on Canada, *Portraits of Canada*, online: <http://www.cric.ca/en_re/portraits/index.html> (date accessed: 19 December 2003).

Courtney, J. C., "Electoral Reform and Canada's Parties" in H. Milner, ed., *Making Every Vote Count: Reassessing Canada's Electoral System* (Peterborough: Broadview Press, 1999) 91.

Courtney, J. C., "Is Talk of Electoral Reform Just Whistling in the Wind?" (2001) 22:6 *Policy Options* 17.

Cousins, J. A., *Electoral Reform for Prince Edward Island: A Discussion Paper* (Charlottetown: Institute of Island Studies at the University of Prince Edward Island, 2000).

Dinan, D., *Ever Closer Union? An Introduction to the European Community* (Boulder: Lynne Reiner Publishers, 1994).

Derriennic, J.-P., "Un systeme électoral adapté aux besoins du Canada" (1997) 18:9 *Policy Options* 6.

Dobell, P., "What Could Canadians Expect from a Minority Government?" (2000) 1:6 *Policy Matters*.

Dunleavy, P. and Margetts, H., "Understanding the Dynamics of Electoral Reform" (1995) 16 *International Political Science Review* 9.

Dunleavy, P., Margetts, H. and Weir, S., *The Politico's Guide to Electoral Reform In Britain* (London: Politicos, 1998).

Dupuis, J. P., Leader parlementaire du gouvernement Ministre délégué à la Réforme des institutions démocratiques et Ministre responsable de la région des Laurentides et de la région de Lanaudière (prepared for delivery at the IRPP Conference: The Reform of Democratic Institutions II, Montreal, 10 September 2003). Online: <http://www.irpp.org/po/index.htm. (date accessed: 30 January 2004).

Earles, K. and T. Findlay, *Rethinking Representation: Toward Democratic Governance in Canada* (Ottawa: Law Commission of Canada, 2003).

Elections Canada, National Forum on Youth Voting (30–31 October 2003), Report, online: <http://www.elections.ca/content.asp?section= med&document=rep&dir=eveyou/forum&lang=e&textonly=false> (date accessed: 24 February 2004).

Elections Canada, Press Releases and Media Advisories, 21 March and 30 October 2003, online: <http://www.elections.ca/content.asp?section= med&document=index&dir=pre&lang=e&textonly=false> (date accessed: 19 December 2003).

Elections New Zealand, "Maori and the Vote" online: <http://www.elections.org. nz/elections/pandr/vote/maori-seats.html> (date accessed: 19 December 2003).

Elections New Zealand, "New Zealand's Electoral System: How Parliament is Elected," online: <http://www.elections.org.nz/elections/esyst/govt_ elect.html> (date accessed: 5 January 2004).

Electoral Reform Society, *French Presidential Election 2002: Failings of the Second Ballot System* (London, 2002).

Equal Voice, "Equality-Based Electoral Reform" online: <http://www.equal voice.ca/index.htm> (date accessed: 10 September 2003).

Fair Vote Canada, "Dubious Democracy Report", online: <http://www.fairvote canada.org/updir/Dubious_Democracy_Report.pdf> (date accessed: December 15, 2003).

Farrell, D. M., *Comparing Electoral Systems* (London: Prentice Hall, 1997).

Federal Elections Boundaries Commission for New Brunswick, *Proposed Boundaries*, online: <http://www.elections.ca/scripts/fedrep/newbruns/ proposals/boundaries_e.htm> (date accessed: 3 March 2004).

Figueroa v. Canada (Attorney General), [2003] 1 S.C.R., No. 28194 (S.C.C.).

Flanagan, T., "The Alternative Vote: An Electoral System for Canada." in H. Milner, ed., *Making Every Vote Count: Reassessing Canada's Electoral System* (Peterborough: Broadview Press, 1999) 85.

Fleras, A., "Aboriginal Electoral Districts for Canada: Lessons from New Zealand" in R. Milen, ed., *Aboriginal Peoples and Electoral Reform in*

Canada, Vol. 9 of the Research Studies for the Royal Commission on Electoral Reform and Party Financing (Toronto: Dundurn Press, 1991) 67.

Gibbins, R., "Electoral Reform and Canada's Aboriginal Population: An Assessment of Aboriginal Electoral Districts" in R. Milen, ed., *Aboriginal Peoples and Electoral Reform in Canada,* Vol. 9 of the Research Studies for the Royal Commission on Electoral Reform and Party Financing (Toronto: Dundurn Press, 1991).

Gibson, G., *Report on the Constitution of the Citizens' Assembly on Electoral Reform* (Vancouver, 23 December 2002).

Gidengil, E., Blais, A., Nevitte, N. and Nadeau, R., "Turned Off or Tuned Out? Youth Participation in Politics" (2003) 5:2 *Electoral Insight* 9.

The Globe and Mail, "Suppose the outcome reflected all the votes." (16 October 2003) (Editorial) at A26.

Hansard (Edited), Number 012: Motion No. 398 (17 February 2004), 37th Parliament, 3rd Session.

Harper v. Canada (Attorney General) [2002] (A.J.) No. 1542 (A.B.C.A.).

Harris, P., "New Zealand Adopts PR: A Research Director's View" (2001) 22:6 *Policy Options* 31.

Horowitz, D. L., "Electoral Systems: A Primer For Decision Makers" (2003) 14:4 *Journal of Democracy* 5.

Henderson, A. "Practical Consequences of Electoral Reform: International Lessons" (paper presented to the Annual Meeting of the Canadian Association of Law Teachers, Toronto, 25 June 2002).

Howe, P. and Northrup, D., "Strengthening Canadian Democracy: The Views of Canadians" (2000) 1:5 *Policy Matters.*

International Institute for Democracy and Electoral Assistance, "Voter Turnout—A Global Survey", online: <http://www.idea.int/vt/survey/voter_turnout.cfm> (date accessed: 9 August 2003).

International Institute for Democracy and Electoral Assistance, "Electoral System Families", online: <http://www.idea.int/esd/systems.cfm> (date accessed: 19 June 2003).

International Institute for Democracy and Electoral Assistance, "Global Database of Quotas for Women", online: <http://www.idea.int/quota/index.cfm> (date accessed: 23 January 2004).

Inter-Parliamentary Union, "Germany: Electoral System", online: <http://www.ipu.org/parline-e/reports/2121_B.htm> (date accessed: 19 December 2003).

Inter-Parliamentary Union, "Women in National Parliaments: Situation as of 31 May 2003", online: <http://www.ipu.org/wmn-e/classif.htm> (date accessed: 16 September 2003).

Irvine, W. P., *Does Canada Need a New Electoral System?* (Kingston: Institute of Intergovernmental Relations, Queen's University, 1979).

Irvine, W. P., "A Review and Evaluation of Electoral System Reform Proposals" in P. Aucoin, ed., *Institutional Reforms for Representative Government*, Vol. 38 of the Research Studies commissioned for the Royal Commission on the Economic Union and Development Prospects for Canada (Toronto: University of Toronto Press, 1985) 71.

Johnston, R., "Canadian Elections at the Millennium" (2000) 6:6 *Choices: Strengthening Canadian Democracy* 4.

Johnston, R., "A Conservative Case for Electoral Reform" (2001) 22:6 *Policy Options* 7.

Jones, M. P., and Navia, P., "Assessing the Effectiveness of Gender Quotas in Open-List Proportional Representation Electoral Systems" (1999) 80:2 *Social Science Quarterly* 341.

Karp, J., and Bowler, S., "Coalition Politics and Satisfaction with Democracy: Explaining New Zealand's Reaction to Proportional Representation" (2001) 40:1 *European Journal of Political Research* 57.

Katz, R. S., "Electoral Reform is not as Simple as it Looks" in H. Milner, ed., *Making Every Vote Count: Reassessing Canada's Electoral System* (Peterborough: Broadview Press, 1999) 101.

Katz, R. S., "Reforming the Italian Electoral Law, 1993" in M. S. Shugart and M. P. Wattenberg, eds., *Mixed Member Electoral Systems: The Best of Both Worlds?* (Oxford: Oxford University Press, 2001) 96.

Keenan, D., "The New Zealand Wars" online: <http://www.newzealand wars.co.nz> (date accessed: 19 December 2003).

Kent, T., "How to Renew Canadian Democracy: PR for the Commons, FPTP Elections for the Senate, and Political Financing for Individuals Only" in H. Milner, ed., *Making Every Vote Count: Reassessing Canada's Electoral System* (Peterborough: Broadview Press, 1999) 51.

Klingemann, H.-D., and Wessels, B., "The Political Consequences of Germany's Mixed-Member System: Personalization at the Grass Roots?" in M. S. Shugart and M. P. Wattenberg, eds., *Mixed Member Electoral Systems: The Best of Both Worlds?* (Oxford: Oxford University Press, 2001) 279.

Knight, T., "Unconstitutional Democracy? A Charter Challenge to Canada's Electoral System" (1999) 57:1 *University of Toronto Faculty Law Review* 1.

Knight, T., "Electoral Justice for Aboriginal People in Canada" (2001) 46 *McGill L.J.* 1063.

Leduc, L., "New Challenges Require New Thinking about our Antiquated Electoral System" in H. Milner, ed., *Making Every Vote Count: Reassessing Canada's Electoral System* (Peterborough: Broadview Press, 1999) 63.

Lemieux, V., "Le Vote Unique Transférable" (1997) 18:9 *Policy Options* 6.

Levine, S., and Roberts, N.S., "MMP: The Decision" in R. Miller, ed., *New Zealand Politics in Transition* (Auckland: Oxford University Press, 1997) 25.

Lijphart, A., "Trying to Have the Best of Both Worlds: Semi-Proportional and Mixed Systems" in A. Lijphart and B. Grofman, eds., *Choosing an Electoral System: Issues and Alternatives* (New York: Praeger, 1984) 207.

Lijphart, A., *Electoral Systems and Party Systems: A Study of Twenty-Seven Democracies, 1945–1990* (Oxford: Oxford University Press, 1994).

Lijphart, A., *Patterns of Democracy: Government Forms and Performance in Thirty-Six Countries* (New Haven: Yale University Press, 1999).

MacIvor, H., "A Brief Introduction to Electoral Reform" in H. Milner, ed., *Making Every Vote Count: Reassessing Canada's Electoral System* (Peterborough: Broadview Press, 1999) 19.

MacKay, P., "The Progressive Conservative Party's Perspective" (2001) 22:6 *Policy Options* 70.

MacShane, D., "Open Lists Will give Us Closed Minds" (27 November 1998) *The New Statesman* 127.

Marchand, L., "Proportional Representation for Native Peoples" (1990) 13:3 *Canadian Parliamentary Review* 9.

Martin, P., "The Democratic Deficit" (2003) 24:1 *Policy Options* 10.

Massicotte, L., "Changing the Canadian Electoral System" (2001) 7:1 *Choices: Strengthening Canadian Democracy* 3.

Massicotte, L., and Blais, A., "Mixed Electoral Systems: A Conceptual and Empirical Survey" (1998) 18:3 *Electoral Studies* 341.

Mayorga, R. A., "Electoral Reform in Bolivia: Origins of the Mixed-Member Proportional System" in M. S. Shugart and M. P. Wattenberg, eds., *Mixed Member Electoral Systems: The Best of Both Worlds* (Oxford: Oxford University Press, 2001) 194.

McPhedran, M., with Speirs, R., "Reducing the Democratic Deficit Through Equality Based Electoral Reform" (paper submitted to the Law Commission of Canada, Spring 2003).

Mendelsohn, M., Parkin, A., and Van Kralingen, A., "Getting from Here to There: A Process for Electoral Reform in Canada" (2001) 22:6 *Policy Options* 55.

Milner, H., "Obstacles to Electoral Reform in Canada" (1994) 24:1 *The American Review of Canadian Studies* 39.

Milner, H., "The Case for Proportional Representation" (1997) 18:9 *Policy Options* 6.

Milner, H., "The Case for Proportional Representation in Canada" in H. Milner, ed., Making Every Vote Count: Reassessing Canada's Electoral System (Peterborough: Broadview Press, 1999) 37.

Milner, H., ed., *Making Every Vote Count: Reassessing Canada's Electoral System* (Peterborough: Broadview Press, 1999).

New Democratic Party of Canada, Proportional Representation Committee. "Report to Convention" (Toronto, 24–26 January 2003).

New Democratic Party of Ontario, "Publicpower: Practical Solutions for Ontario" (2003).

New Zealand, Royal Commission on the Electoral System. *Towards a Better Democracy* (Wellington: Government Printer, 1986).

Niemczak, P., *Aboriginal Political Representation: A Review of Several Jurisdictions* (Ottawa: Library of Parliament, Research Branch, 1994).

Ontario Liberal Party, "Government That Works for You: The Ontario Liberal Plan for a More Democratic Ontario" (April 2003).

Ontario, Ministry of the Attorney General and Democratic Renewal Secretariat, News Release (8 December 2003).

Pammett, J. and LeDuc, L., "Confronting the Problem of Declining Voter Turnout Among Youth" (2003) 5:2 *Electoral Insight* 3.

Paul Martin Times, online: <www.paulmartin.ca> "Martin Announces Detailed Plan for New Government", 12 December 2003 (date accessed: 19 December 2003).

Pilon, D., "The History of Voting System Reform In Canada" in H. Milner, ed., *Making Every Vote Count: Reassessing Canada's Electoral System* (Peterborough: Broadview Press, 1999) 111.

Pilon, D., "Renewing Canadian Democracy: Citizen Engagement in Voting System Reform" (Ottawa: Law Commission of Canada, March 2003).

Pond, D., "Guaranteed Aboriginal Seats in Legislatures" *Current Issue Paper #127* (Toronto: Legislative Research Service, 1992).

Prince Edward Island Electoral Reform Commission, *Report* (2003).

Progressive Conservative Party of New Brunswick, *Reaching Higher, Going Further* (2003).

Québec, Assemblée nationale, "Conférence de presse de M. Jean-Pierre Charbonneau, Ministre responsable de la Réforme des institutions démocratiques; presentation officielle des membres du Comité directeur des états généraux sur la réforme des institutions démocratiques" (5 September 2002), online: <http://www.assnat.qc.ca/fra/conf-presse/020905jp.htm> (date accessed: 26 January 2004).

Québec, Comité directeur des État Généraux sur la réforme des institutions démocratiques, *Prenez Votre Place! La participation citoyenne au coeur des institutions démocratiques québécoises* (2003).

Québec, Ministre d'État à la Réforme électorale et parlementaire, *One Citizen, One Vote: Green Paper on the Reform of the Electoral System* (Éditeur official du Québec, 1979).

Quebec Liberal Party, "Making Voting System Reform a Priority" (brief presented to the Steering Committee for the General Consultation on the Reform of the Voting System of Quebec, November 2002).

Quebec Liberal Party, "A Necessary Reform of the Voting System" (brief presented to the Committee of Institutions of the National Assembly, November 2002).

Rebick, J. "PR Can Help Solve Canada's Democracy Deficit" (July–August 2001) *Policy Options* 16.

Reed, S. R., and Thies, M.F., "The Consequences of Electoral Reform in Japan" in M. S. Shugart and M. P. Wattenberg, eds., *Mixed Member Electoral Systems: The Best of Both Worlds?* (Oxford: Oxford University Press, 2001) 380.

Referendum Act, R.S.C. 1992, c. 30.

Reynolds, A. and Reilly, B., *The International IDEA Handbook of Electoral System Design*, 2nd ed. (Stockholm: International Institute for Democracy and Electoral Assistance, 1997).

Roberts, N., "New Zealand: A Long-Established Westminster Democracy Switches to PR" in A. Reynolds and B. Reilly, eds., *The International IDEA Handbook of Electoral System Design*, 2nd ed. (Stockholm: International Institute for Democracy and Electoral Assistance, 1997) 129.

Ruff, N., "BC Deliberative Democracy: The Citizens' Assembly and Electoral Reform 2003–2005" (paper presented to the annual conference of the Canadian Political Science Association, Halifax, 1 June 2003).

Russow v. Canada (A.G.), Court File No. 01-CV-210088 (Ont. S.C.J.). Supporting documentation available at the website of the University of Toronto Test Case Centre: <http://www.law-lib.utoronto.ca/testcase/> (date accessed: 26 January 2004).

Savoie, D., *Governing from the Centre: The Concentration of Power in Canadian Politics* (Toronto: University of Toronto Press, 1999).

Schmidt, J., *Aboriginal Representation in Government: A Comparative Examination* (Ottawa: Law Commission of Canada, 2003).

Schouls, T., "Aboriginal Peoples and Electoral Reform in Canada: Differentiated Representation Versus Voter Equality" (1996) 29 *Canadian Journal of Political Science* 729.

Schwartz, B. and Rettie, D., "Valuing Canadians: The Options for Voting System Reform in Canada" (Ottawa: Law Commission of Canada, 2002).

The Scottish Parliament, "Elections and the Electoral System", online: <http://www.scottish.parliament.uk/> (date accessed: 21 October 2003).

Seidle, F. L., "The Canadian Electoral System and Proposals for Reform" in A. Brian Tanguay and A.-G. Gagnon, eds., *Canadian Parties in Transition*, 2nd ed. (Scarborough: Nelson, 1996) 282.

Seidle, F. L., "Electoral System Reform in Canada: Objectives, Advocacy and Implications for Governance." (Ottawa: Canadian Policy Research Networks Inc., 2002).

Shugart, M. S., and Wattenberg, M.P., "Conclusion: Are Mixed-Member Systems the Best of Both Worlds?" in M. S. Shugart and M. P. Wattenberg, eds., *Mixed Member Electoral Systems: The Best of Both Worlds?* (Oxford: Oxford University Press, 2001) 571.

Shugart, M. S., and Wattenberg, M.P., "Mixed-Member Systems: A Definition and Typology" in M. S. Shugart and M. P. Wattenberg, eds., *Mixed Member Electoral Systems: The Best of Both Worlds?* (Oxford: Oxford University Press, 2001) 9.

Simard, C., "Political Participation by Ethnocultural Groups and Visible Minorities" 5:2 *Horizons* 2002 at 10.

Simard, C., "Les minorities visibles et le système politique canadien" in Kathy Megyery (ed.), *Ethnocultural Groups and Visible Minorities in Canadian Politics : The Question of Access*, Vol. 7, Royal Commission on Electoral Reform and Party Financing (Toronto: Dundurn Press, 1991) 179–295.

Simpson, J., *The Friendly Dictatorship* (Toronto: McClelland & Stewart, 2001).

Studlar, D., "Will Canada Seriously Consider Electoral Reform? Women and Aboriginals Should" in H. Milner, ed., *Making Every Vote Count: Reassessing Canada's Electoral System* (Peterborough: Broadview Press, 1999) 123.

Sweden, Press and Information Department, Ministry for Foreign Affairs, *Swedish Election Guide 2002* (Edita Norstedts Trykeri, AB, Stolckholm, 2002) at 18, available online at <http://www.utrikes.regeringen.se/inenglish/projects/election_guide/> (date accessed: 15 January 2004).

Taagepera, R., and Shugart, M.S., *Seats and Votes* (New Haven and London: Yale University Press, 1989).

Tanguay, A. B., "Canada's Political Parties in the 1990s: The Fraying of the Ties that Bind" in H. Lazar and T. McIntosh, eds., *Canada: The State of the Federation 1998/99: How Canadians Connect* (Montreal and Kingston: McGill-Queen's University Press, 1999) 217.

Tanguay, A. B., "Political Parties and Canadian Democracy: Making Federalism Do the Heavy Lifting" in H. Bakvis and G. Skogstad, eds., *Canadian Federalism: Performance, Effectiveness, and Legitimacy* (Toronto: Oxford University Press, 2002) 296.

Tremblay, M. *La Représentation Politique au Canada : sur quelques considérations théoriques et empiriques* (Ottawa : Law Commission of Canada, 2003).

United Kingdom, Independent Commission on the Voting System [Jenkins Commission], *Final Report* (1998).

Vowles, J., "Evaluating Electoral System Change: the Case of New Zealand" (paper prepared for the biennial meeting of the International Political Science Association, Quebec City, 1–5 August 2000).

Vowles, J., Karp, J., and Banducci, S., "Proportional Representation on Trial: Elite vs. Mass Opinion on Electoral System Change in New Zealand" (paper prepared for the annual meeting of the American Political Science Association, Washington, D.C., 30 August– 3 September 2000).

Wales, The National Assembly, "Public Information—Presiding Office. About the Assembly: How the First Assembly was Elected", online: <http://www.wales.gov.uk/pubinfaboutassembly/content/howfirst-e.htm> (date accessed: 21 November 2003).

Ward, L. J., "'Second-Class MPs'? New Zealand's Adaptation to Mixed-Member Parliamentary Representation" (1998) 49:2 *Political Science* 125.

Watt N., "Women win half of Welsh seats," *The Guardian*, Saturday, 3 May 2003. Online:<http://www.politics.guardian.co.uk/wales/story/0,9061,948680,00.html> (date accessed: 23 January 2004).

Wattenberg, M. P., "The Decline of Party Mobilization" in R. J. Dalton and M. P. Wattenberg, eds., *Parties Without Partisans: Political Change in Advanced Industrial Democracies* (New York: Oxford University Press, 2000) 64.

Weaver, K., "A Hybrid Electoral System for Canada" (1997) 18:9 *Policy Options* 3.

Weaver, K., "MMP is Too Much of Some Good Things" in H. Milner, ed., *Making Every Vote Count: Reassessing Canada's Electoral System* (Peterborough: Broadview Press, 1999) 79.

Young, L., *Electoral Systems and Representative Legislatures: Consideration of Alternative Electoral Systems* (Ottawa: Canadian Advisory Council on the Status of Women, 1994).